Ajax and Pickering Ontario in Colour Photos, Saving Our History One Photo at a Time

Photography
by Barbara Raué
©2018

Series Name:
Cruising Ontario

Book 203: Ajax and Pickering

Cover photo: 3590 Mowbray Street, Brougham (Pickering), Page 49

Series Name: Cruising Ontario
Saving Our History One Photo at a Time
in colour photos

Books Available in Alphabetical Order:
Aberfoyle, Acton, Ajax, Alton, Amherstburg, Ancaster, Arthur, Auburn, Aylmer, Ayr, Beaver Valley, Belgrave, Belleville, Bloomingdale, Blyth, Brantford, Brockville, Burford, Burlington, Caledon, Caledonia, Cambridge, Carlow, Chatsworth, Clifford, Collingwood, Conestogo, Delhi, Dorchester to Aylmer, Drayton, Drumbo, Dundas, Dunlop, Eden Mills, Elmira, Elora, Erin, Essex, Fergus, Goderich, Grimsby, Guelph, Hagersville, Hamilton, Hanover, Harriston, Hespeler, Jarvis, Kingston, Kingsville, Kitchener, Lake Superior, Lincoln, Linwood, Listowel, London, Lucknow, Merrickville, Mono, Mount Forest, Mount Pleasant, Neustadt, New Hamburg, Newboro, Newport, Niagara-on-the-Lake, Oakville, Onondaga, Orangeville, Orillia, Oshawa, Owen Sound, Palmerston, Paris, Pelham, Perth, Peterborough, Petrolia, Pickering, Port Colborne, Port Elgin, Portland, Preston, Rockwood, Sarnia, Sault Ste. Marie, Seaforth, Sheffield, Shelburne, Simcoe, Smiths Falls, Smithville, Southampton, St. Catharines, St. George, St. Jacobs, St. Marys, St. Thomas, Stoney Creek, Stratford, Thamesford, Thunder Bay, Tillsonburg, Toronto, Waterdown, Waterford, Waterloo, Welland, Wellesley, West Flamborough, Westport, Whitby, Windsor, Wingham, Woodstock

Book 198: Chatsworth
Book 199: Wingham
Book 200: West Flamborough
Book 201-202: Whitby
Book 203: Ajax, Pickering

Table of Contents

Ajax	Page 6
Historic Pickering Village within the Town of Ajax	Page 7
Pickering	Page 47
Hamlet of Brougham	Page 48
Hamlet of Whitevale	Page 58

Ajax is a town in Durham Region in Southern Ontario, Canada, located in the eastern part of the Greater Toronto Area. The town is named for HMS Ajax, a Royal Navy cruiser that served in World War II. It is about twenty-five kilometers (16 miles) east of Toronto on the shores of Lake Ontario and is bordered by the City of Pickering to the west and north, and the Town of Whitby to the east.

Before the Second World War, Ajax was a rural part of the township of Pickering. The town was established in 1941 when a Defense Industries Limited (D.I.L.) shell plant was constructed and a town site grew around the plant. By 1945 the plant employed over 9,000 people at peak production. It had its own water and sewage treatment plants and fifty kilometers (31 miles) of railroad and 50 kilometers (31 miles) of roads. The entire D.I.L. plant site was about twelve square kilometers (5 square miles).

Pickering is a city located in Southern Ontario, east of Toronto in Durham Region. It was settled by British colonists starting in the 1770s. Many of the smaller rural communities have been preserved and function as provincially significant historic sites and museums.

Whitevale, formerly Majorville, is a community located within the City of Pickering. The community was first settled in the 1820s when John Major built a sawmill; there were many Majors living in the area. Around 1855 Truman P. White bought the saw mill, built a gristmill and a cooperage, and in 1866 built a planing factory. In 1867 he built a large four-story brick woolen mill. The community owed so much of its development and business prosperity to T.P. White that in acknowledgement, it adopted Whitevale as its permanent name. In 1855, Donald McPhee opened the first store.

In 1890 Whitevale contained a stave and heading factory and a barrel factory both owned and operated by the Spink brothers; three general stores, one owned by James Taylor and Donald McPhee; a wagon and carriage factory, operated by the Pollard brothers; a cheese factory, owned and operated by P.R. Hoover and Company; the merchant and tailoring firm of J. Rose and Son; the shoemaker shops of John Allen and D. Moodey; the butcher shop of Israel Burton and the tinsmith shop of S.B. Wigmore. In addition, Whitevale contained two blacksmiths, two wagon shops, a school house, undertakers, harness shop, grist mill, brush factory, grindstone factory, barber shop, three dressmakers, three gardeners, money order and post offices, hotel, brass band, two churches and four lodges.

The Whitevale Heritage Conservation District was established to ensure the preservation and enhancement of the special character of Whitevale. It is dominated by its rural setting and modest vernacular buildings; the hamlet has not changed significantly in character since the late 19th century. The building style in Whitevale is a mixture of typical rural Ontario vernacular architecture combined with Victorian influences and materials in common usage at the time of construction. The overall nineteenth century village character has been retained.

Ajax

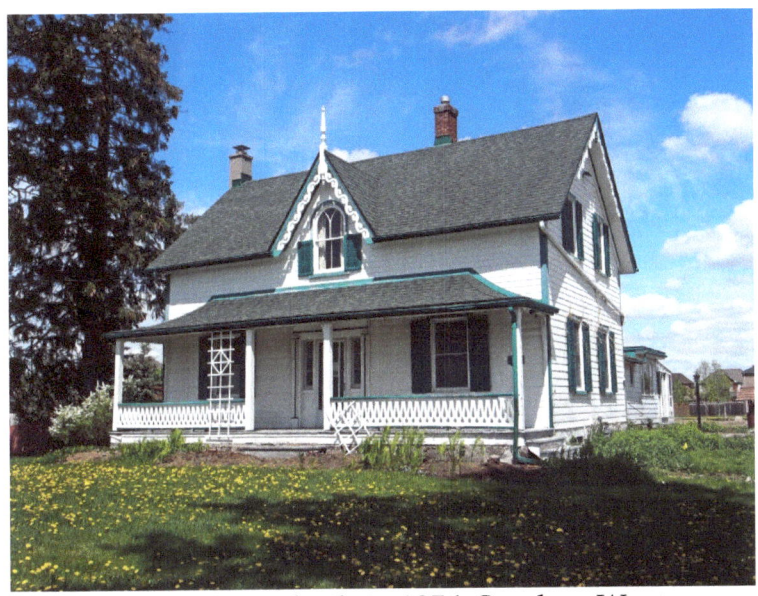

1733 Westney Road was built in 1856. Stephen Westney bought "Maple Dale" farm in 1892. His son William Heron Westney, born on the farm in 1916, served as a Pickering Councilor, and in 1949 was Warden of the County of Ontario. In 1951, the road on which the farm is located was named Westney Road in recognition of his services. William changed the name of the farm to "Westglen" in 1929, which is a combination of the family name and his wife's maiden name (Glendinning).

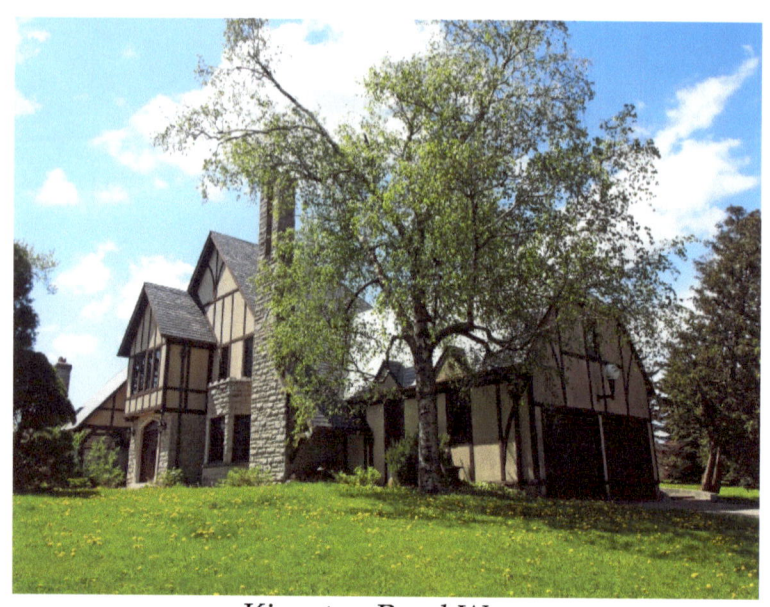

Kingston Road West
Historic Pickering Village within the Town of Ajax

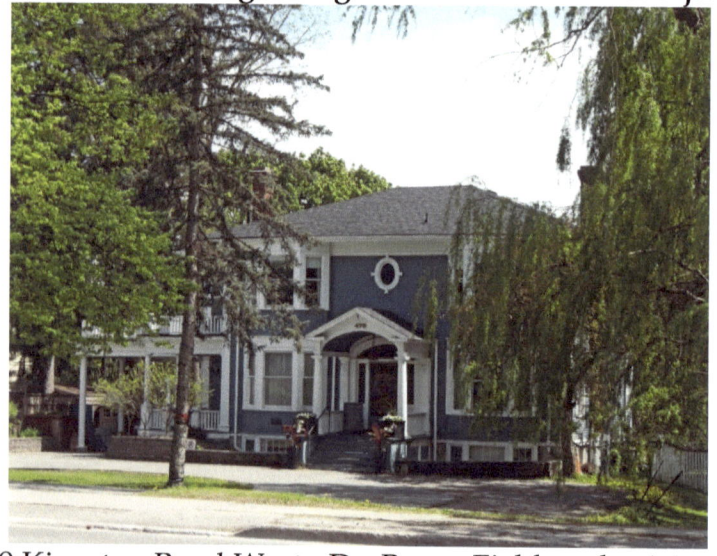

479 Kingston Road West - Dr. Byron Field, a physician in Pickering Village, built this house in 1911. This large two-story frame house, designed by architect A.A. Post, has been carefully maintained and faithfully restored.

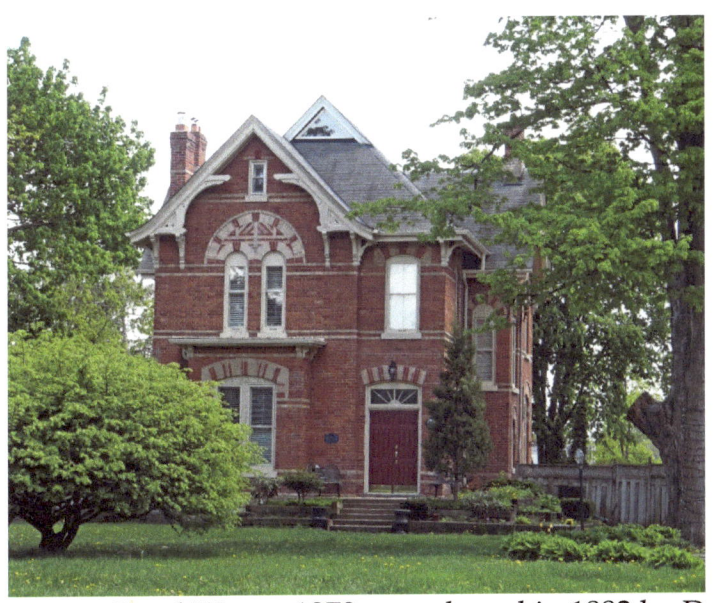

497 Kingston Road West – 1870 - purchased in 1882 by Dr. Field for his daughter. Dr. Field was a practicing physician in Pickering Village and later built his own home directly east of this property. In 1929, Emerson & Henrietta Bertrand purchased the home and raised Allan Irwin. The family gave up the homestead in 1934, only to have it reclaimed in 1977 by their grandson, B. B. Bertrand (son of Allan). The building is a 2½ story brick structure in Italianate architecture.

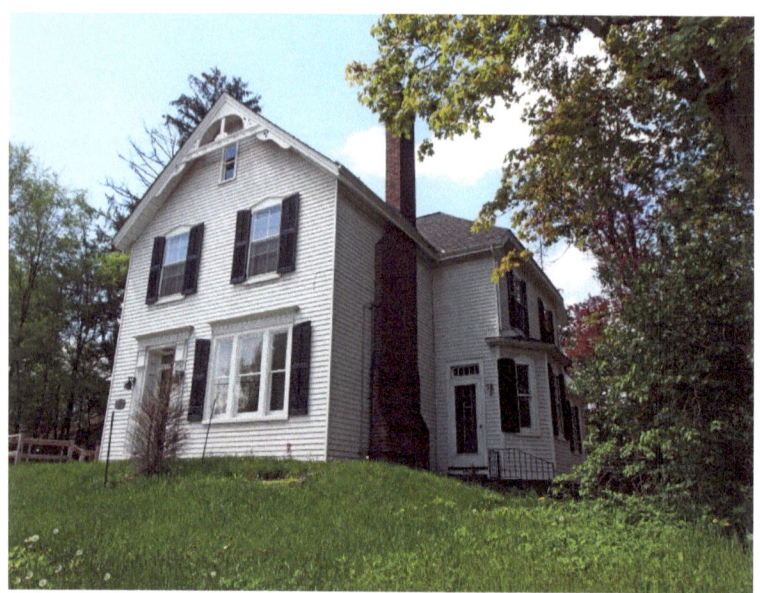

504 Kingston Road West - This home was built in 1890 for the Richardson family, early residents of the Pickering area. As a result of its relatively high perch above street level, the house holds an important place in the streetscape of Kingston Road

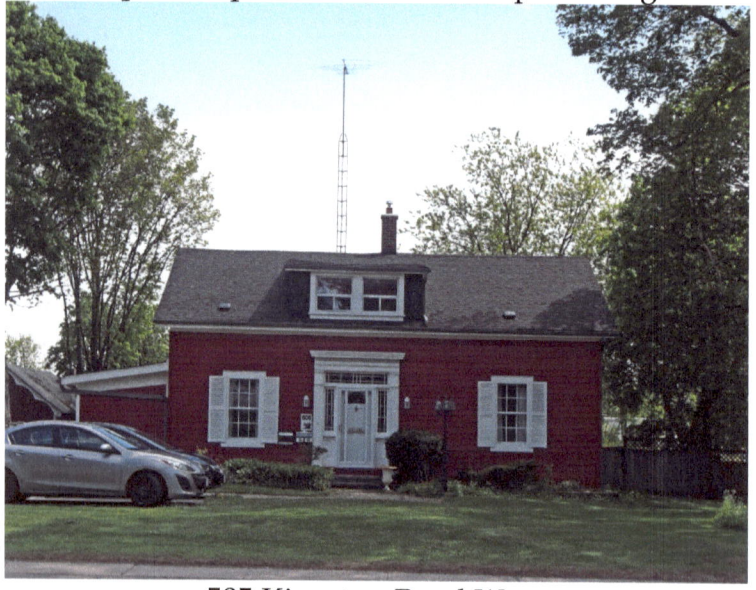

505 Kingston Road West

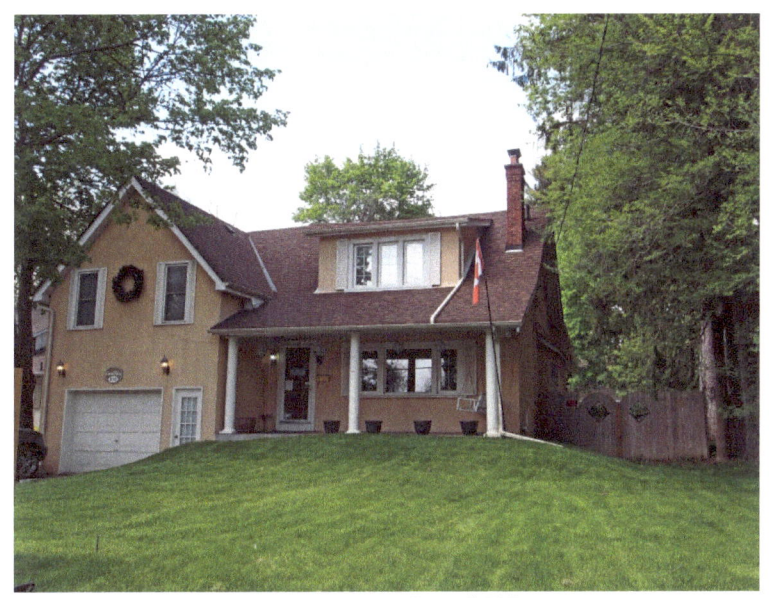

510 Kingston Road West

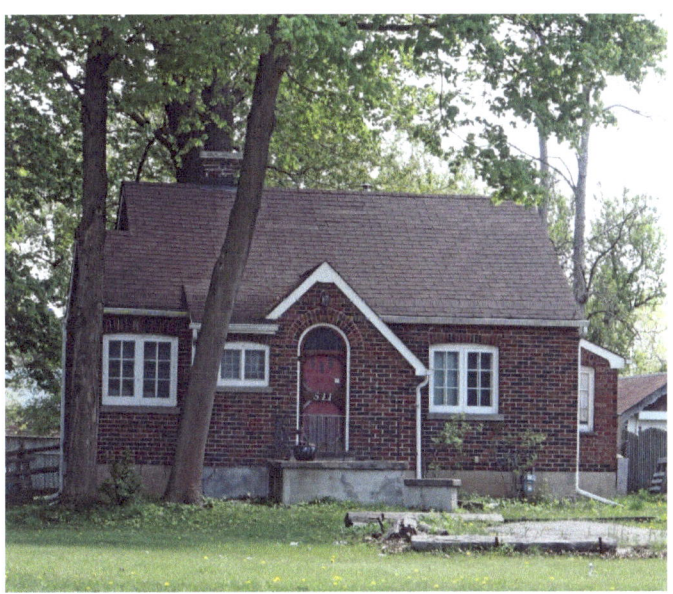

511 Kingston Road West

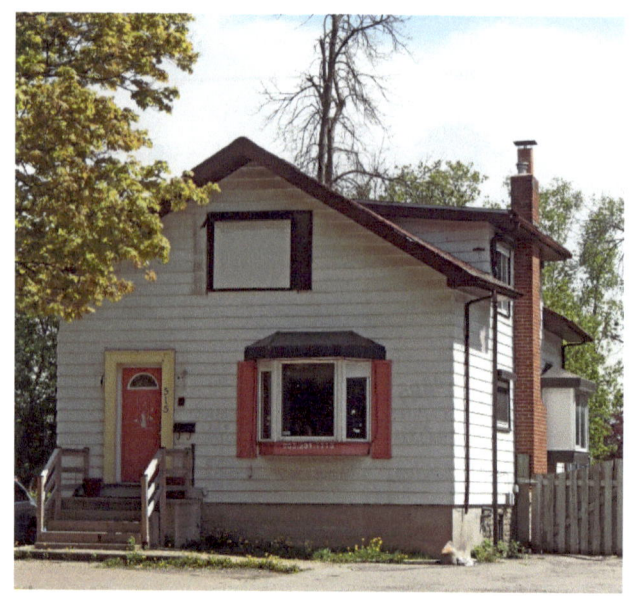
515 Kingston Road West

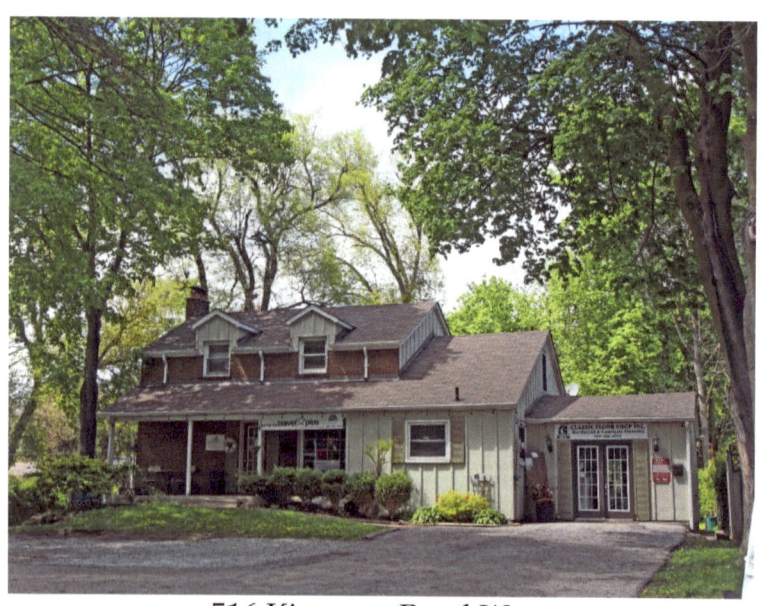
516 Kingston Road West

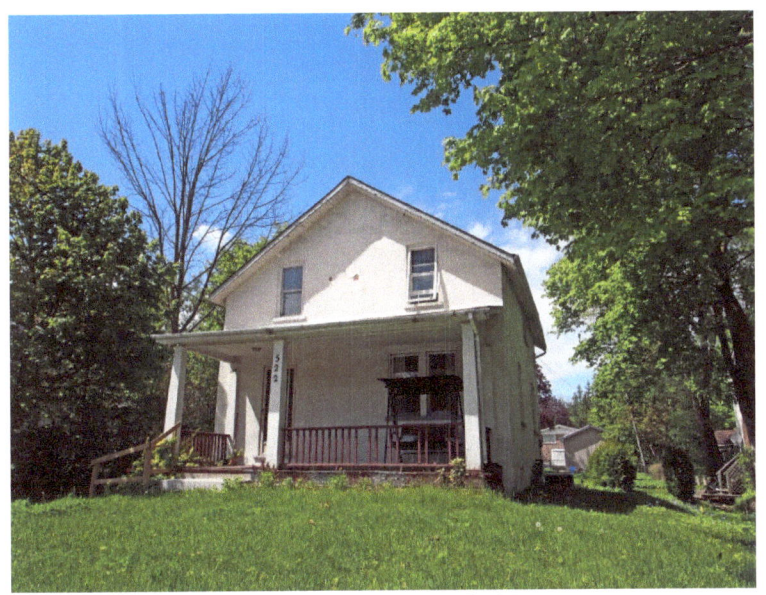

522 Kingston Road West

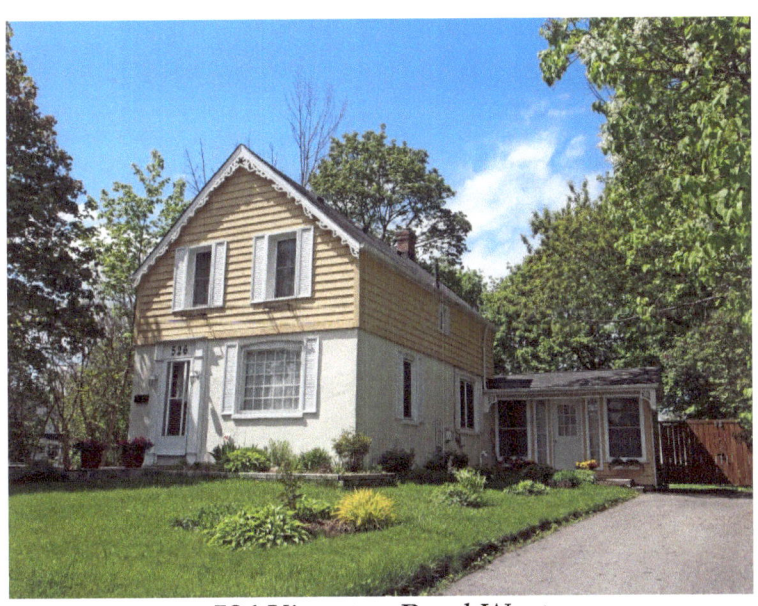

526 Kingston Road West

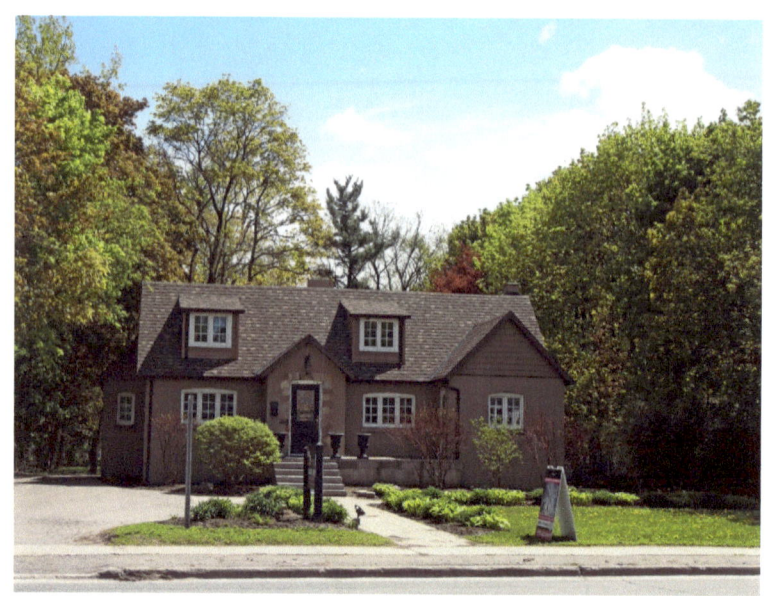

Kingston Road West

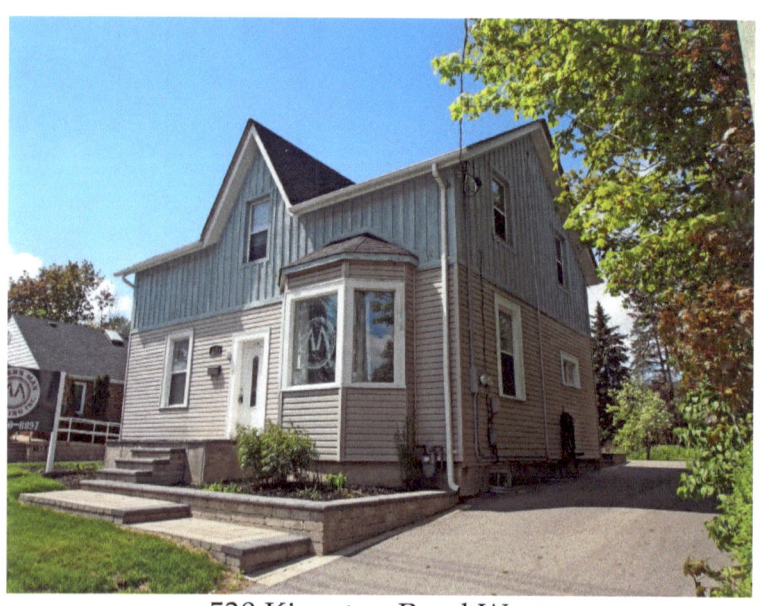

530 Kingston Road West

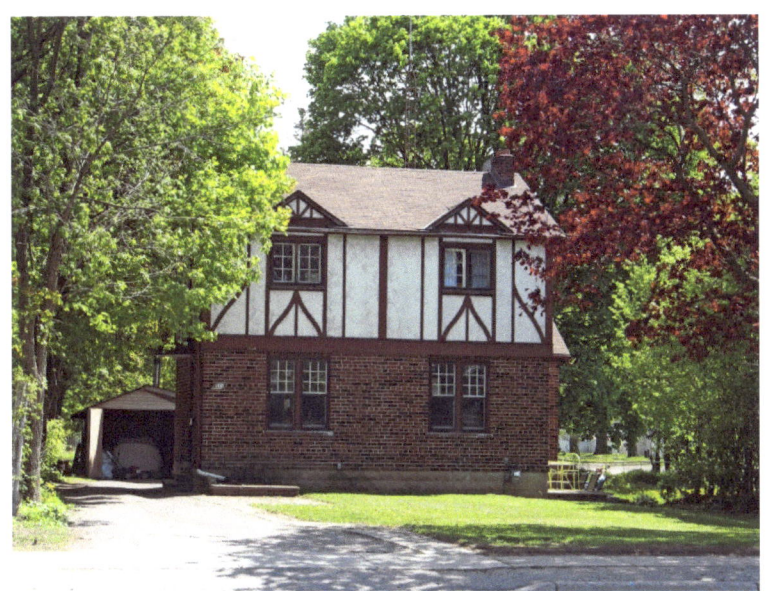

531 Kingston Road West - Tudor

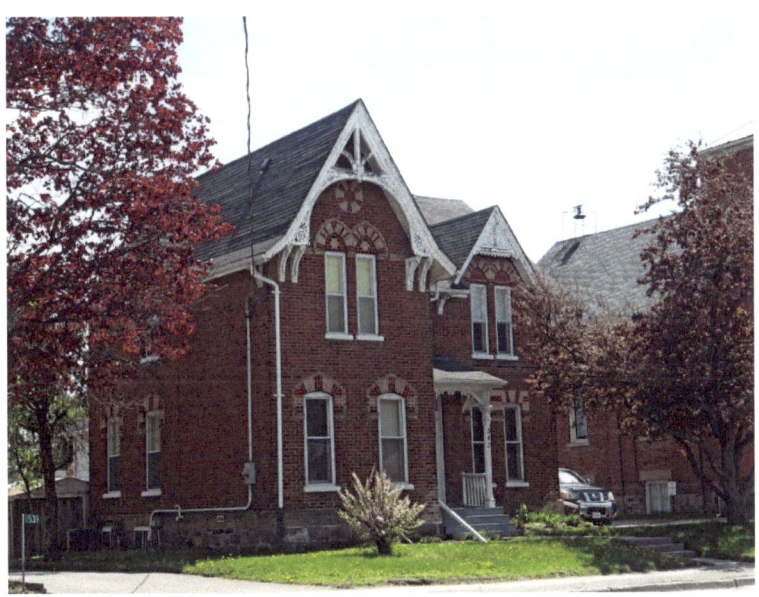

543 Kingston Road West – dichromatic voussoirs

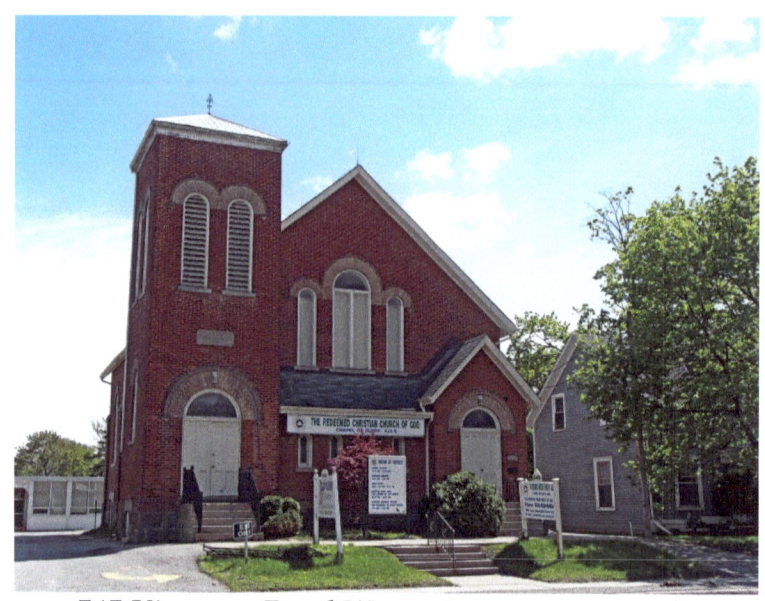
545 Kingston Road West – Romanesque style

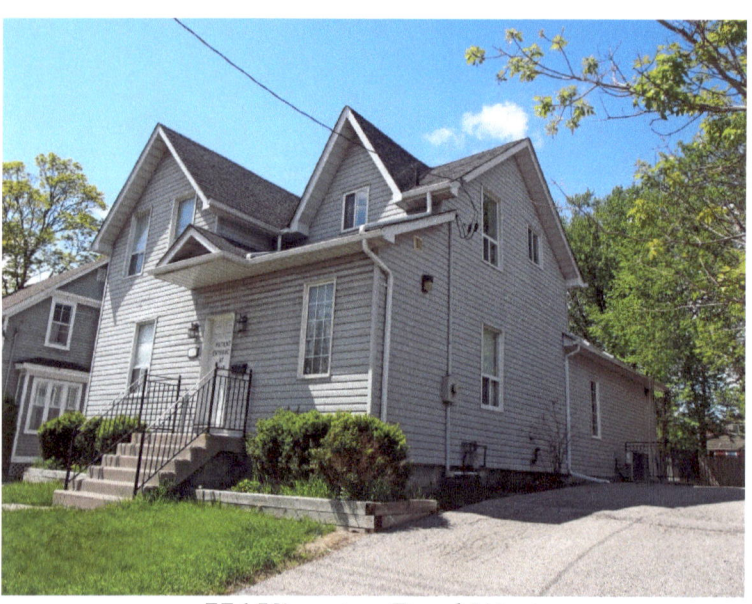
556 Kingston Road West

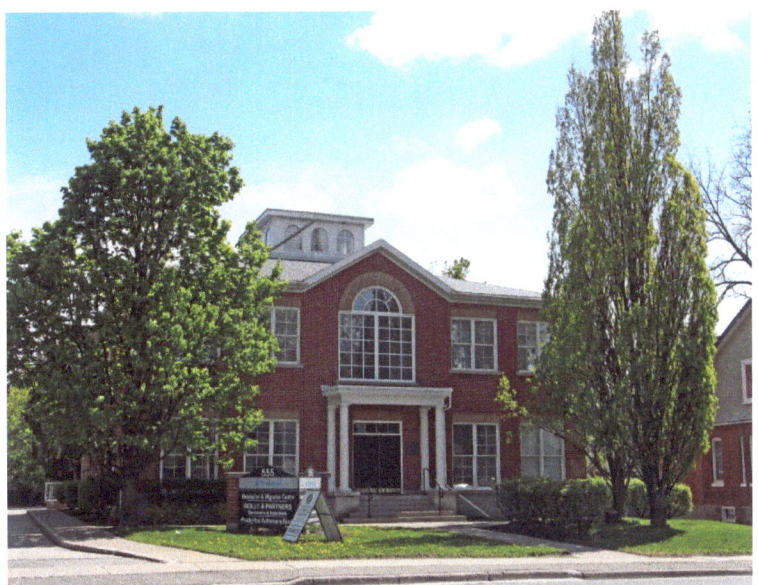

555 Kingston Road West - belvedere

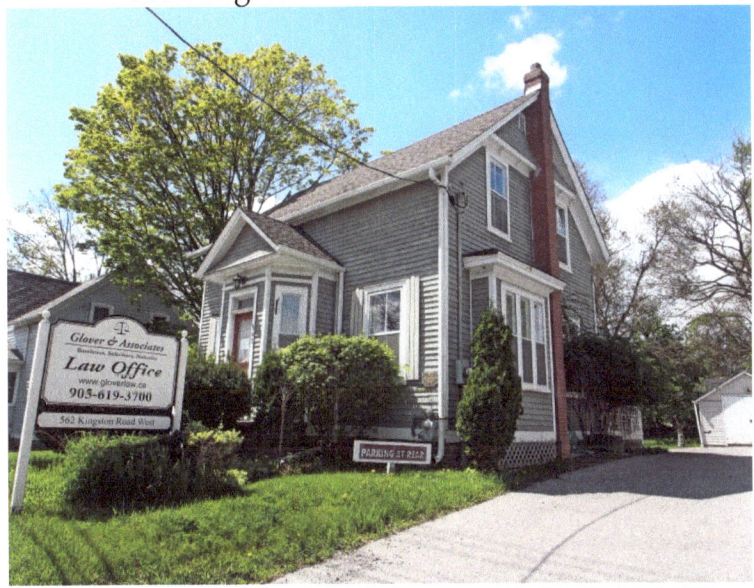

562 Kingston Road West – This house was built in 1870 and is a late Victorian typical merchant/working class dwelling. The frame construction has original narrow wood clapboard with beaded corner boards.

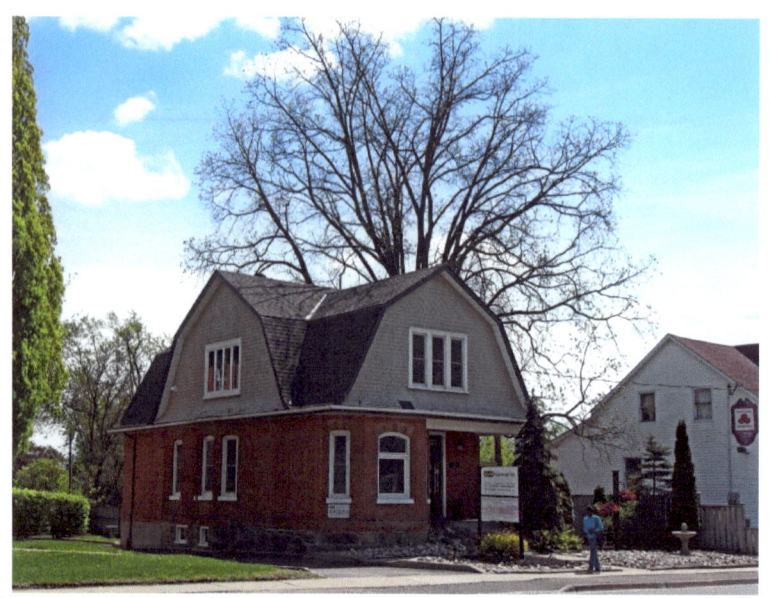
567 Kingston Road West – Dutch Colonial style – gambrel roof

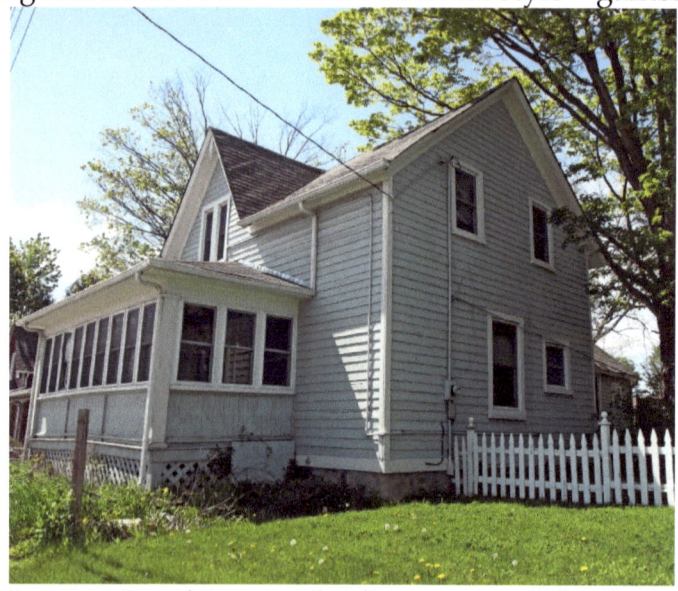
566 Kingston Road West - The first owner of this home was Joseph Ellicott, a member of the Bible Christian Church. It is believed to originally have been a church. Its original clapboard and beaded corner boards remain.

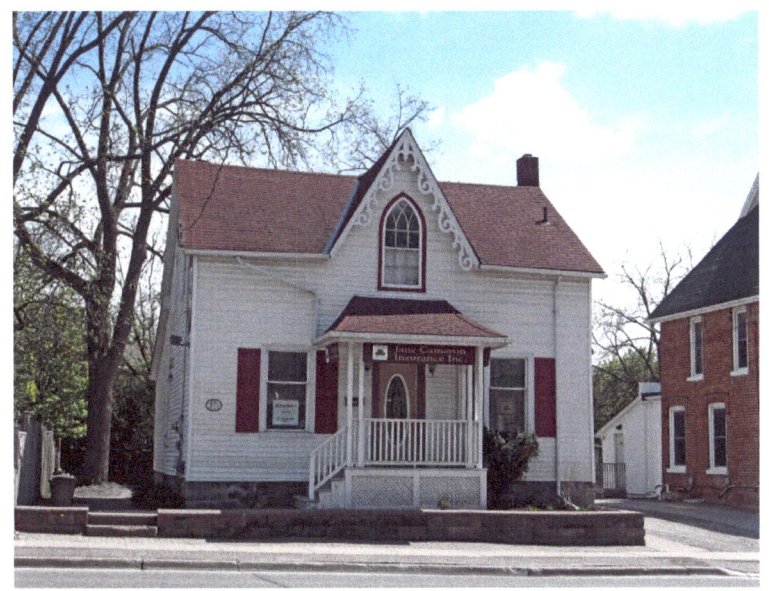

571 Kingston Road West – Gothic, decorative wood fascia

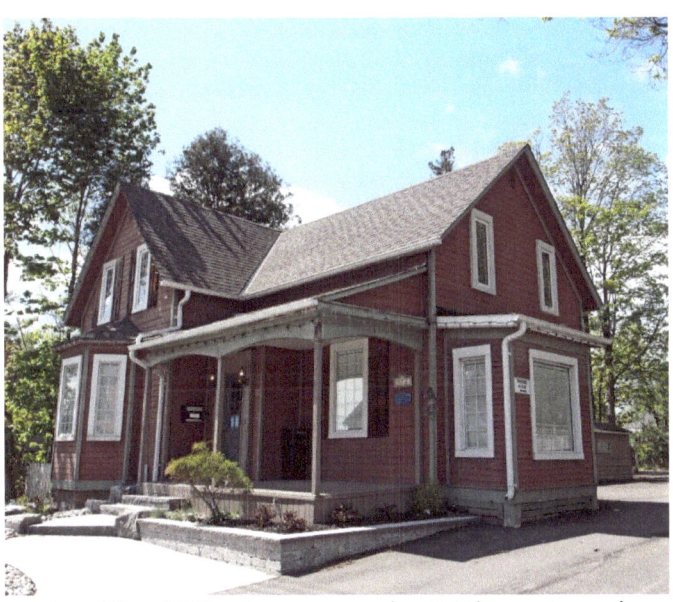

572 Kingston Road West - vernacular 19th century farmhouse

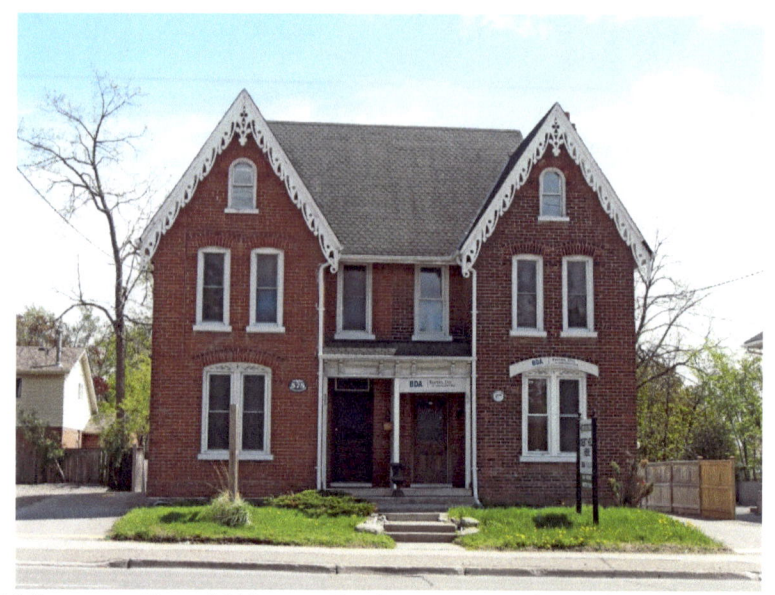

575 Kingston Road West – Gothic – verge board trim on gables

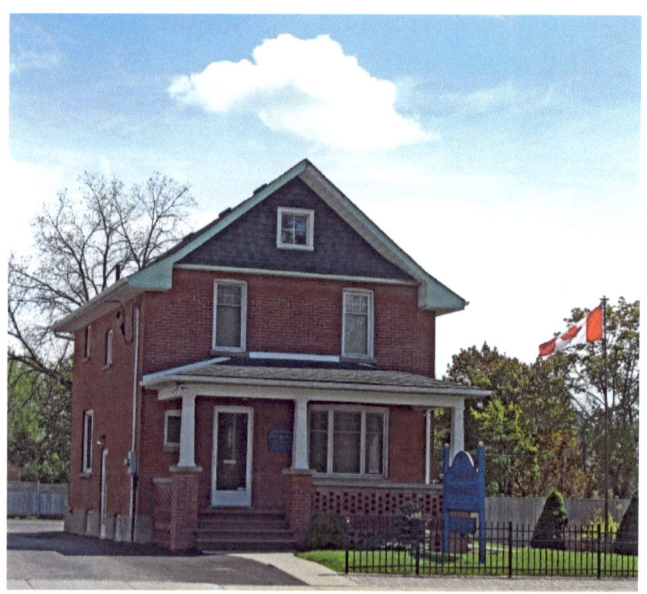

579 Kingston Road West

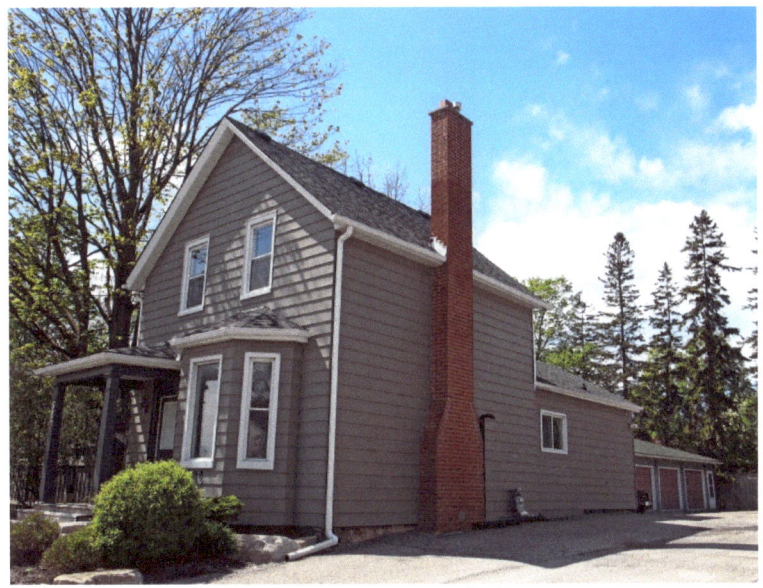

582 Kingston Road West

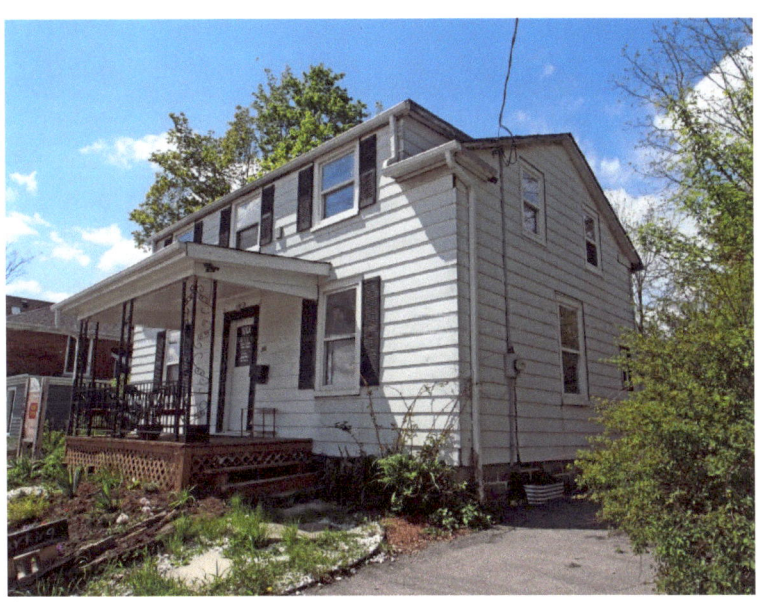

586 Kingston Road West

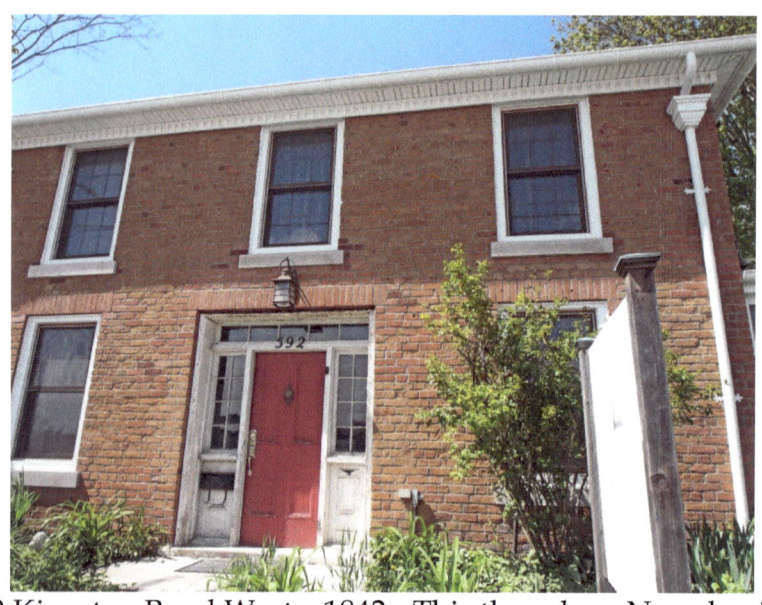

592 Kingston Road West – 1842 - This three-bay, Neo-classical residence known as the Davies House, is the earliest two-story home in Pickering Village. It was originally constructed for a relative of Captain Peter Matthews, a well-known farmer and soldier who was publicly hanged for his participation in the Upper Canada Rebellion of 1837. Subsequent residents were postmaster William Logan and local merchant James Richardson, who operated the nearby Dunbar General Store beginning in 1912.

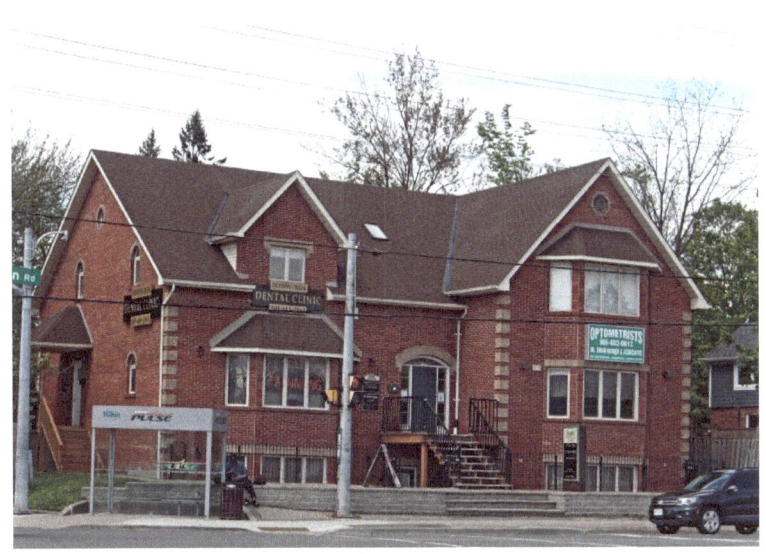

596 Kingston Road West – corner quoins

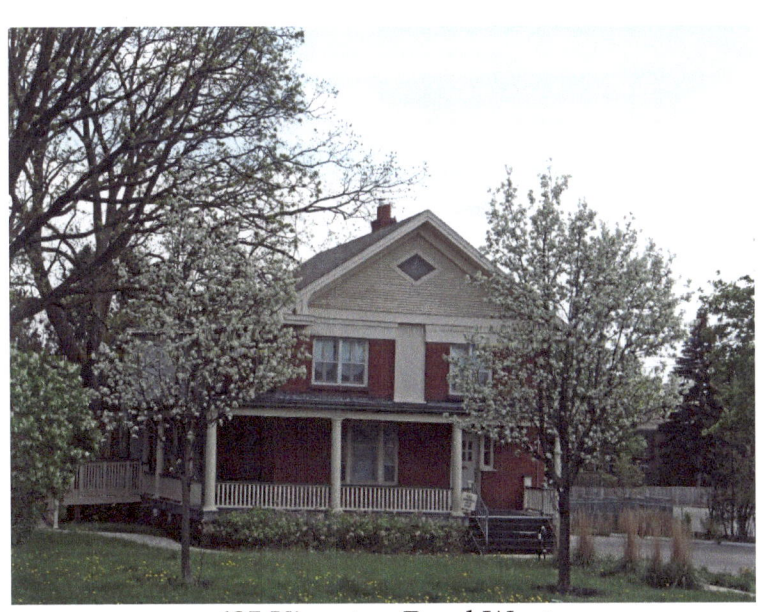

625 Kingston Road West

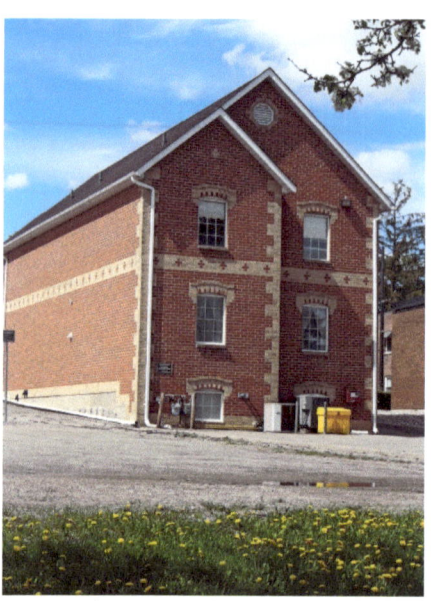
Kingston Road West – banding, corner quoins

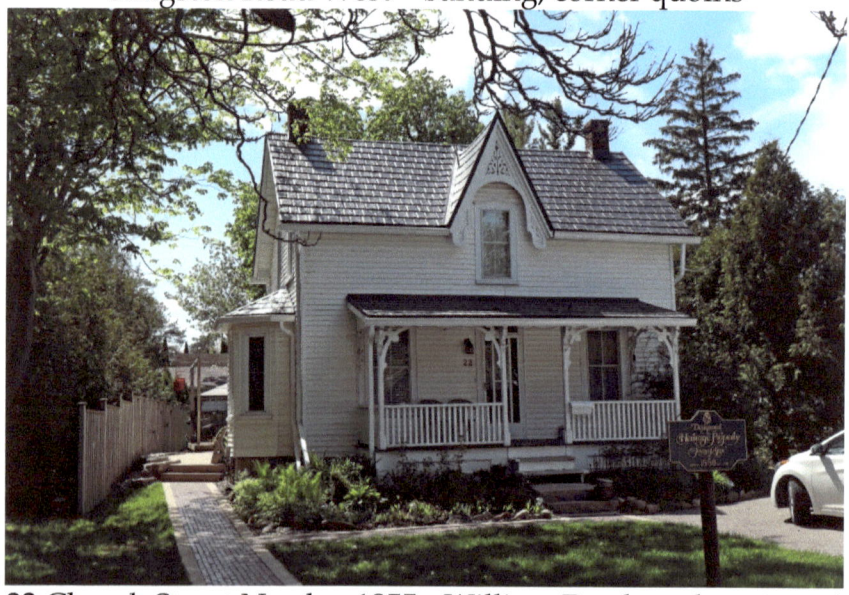
22 Church Street North – 1855 - William Dunbar, the original owner, was a prominent merchant in the years 1880 to 1905, and operated a store at the northwest corner of Church Street and Kingston Road in Pickering Village.

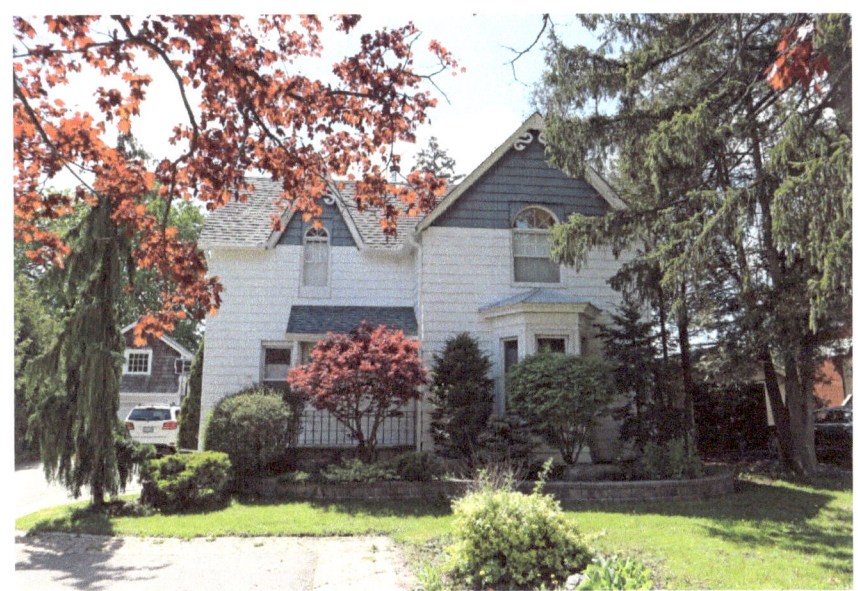

Church Street North

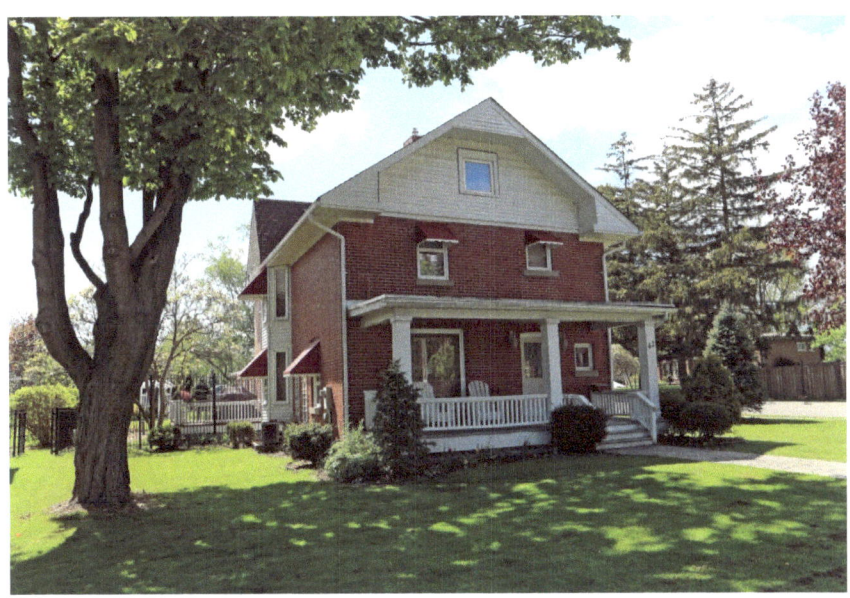

42 Church Street North

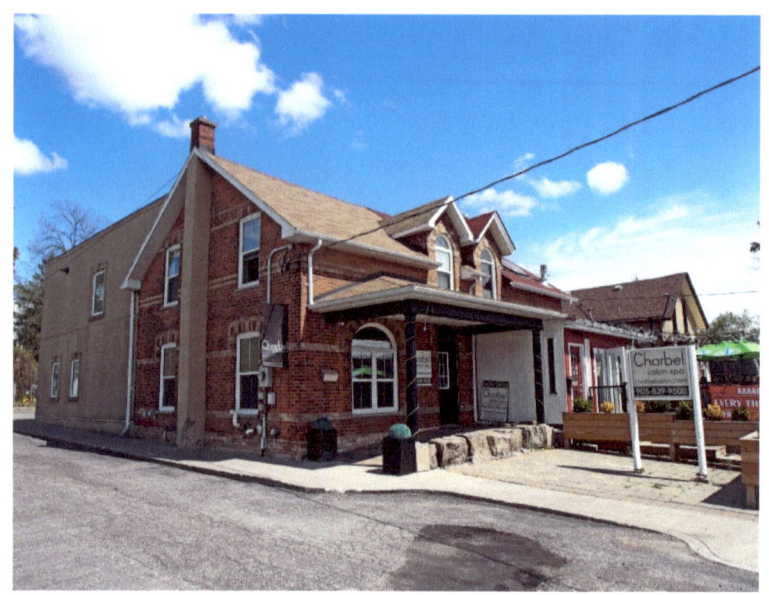
13 Church Street - banding

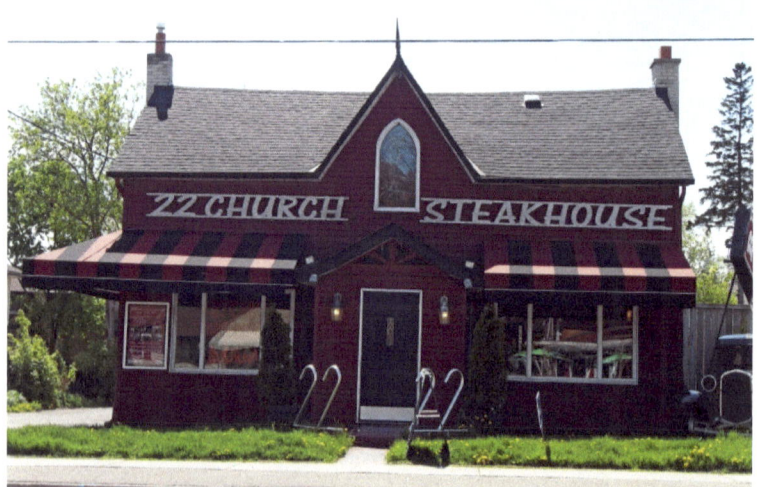
22 Church Street South – Steakhouse - Gothic

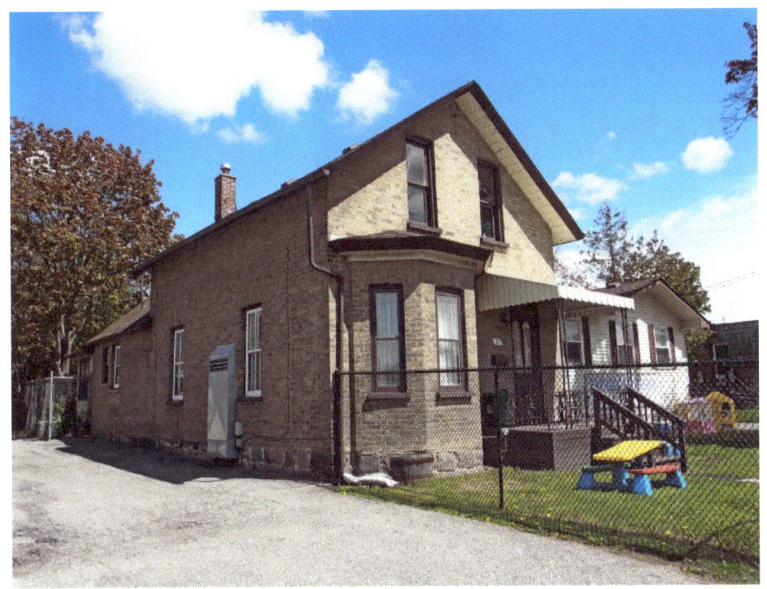

23 Church Street South

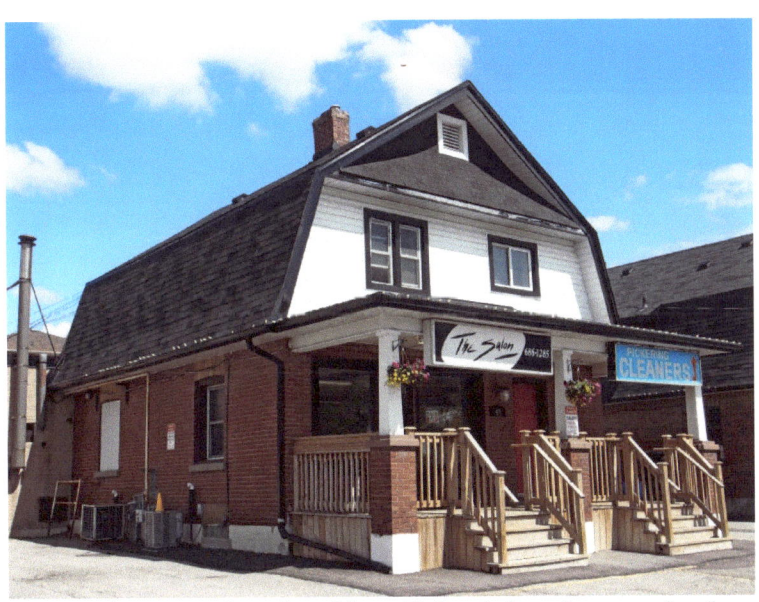

49 Church Street South – Neo-Colonial style, gambrel roof

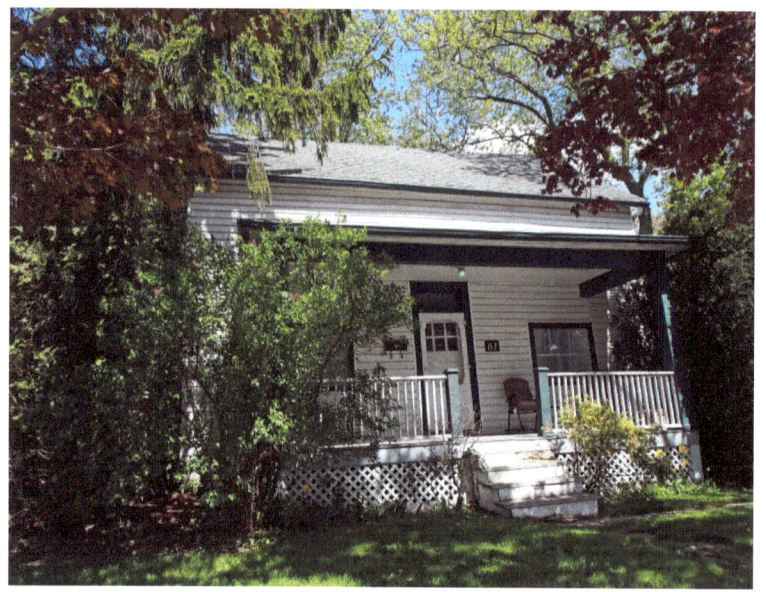
61 Church Street South

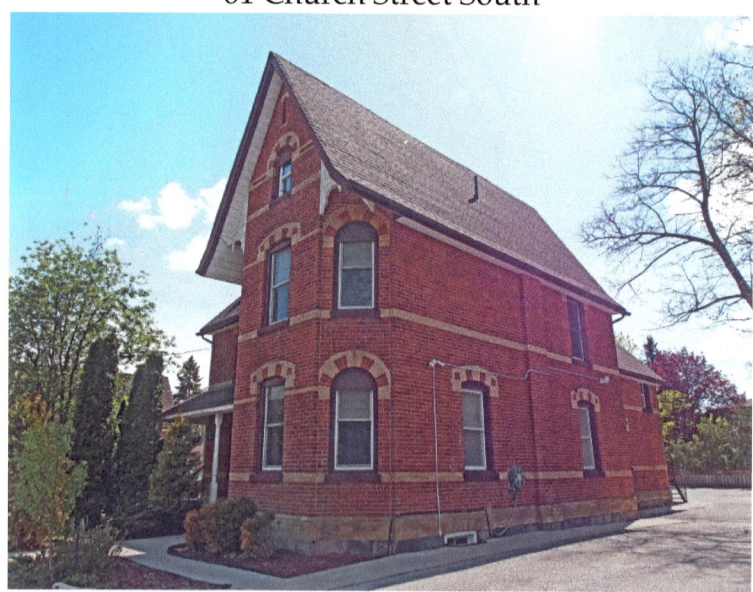
66 Church Street South – dichromatic brickwork, banding

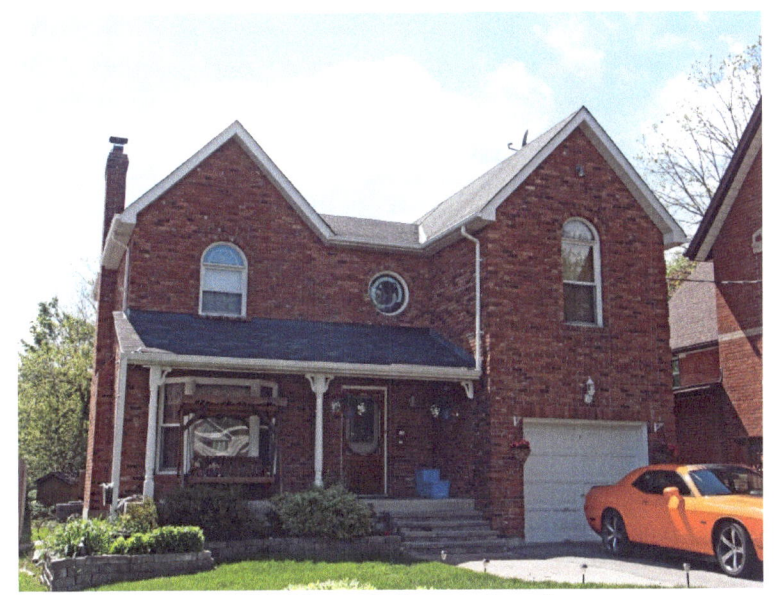

66½ Church Street South

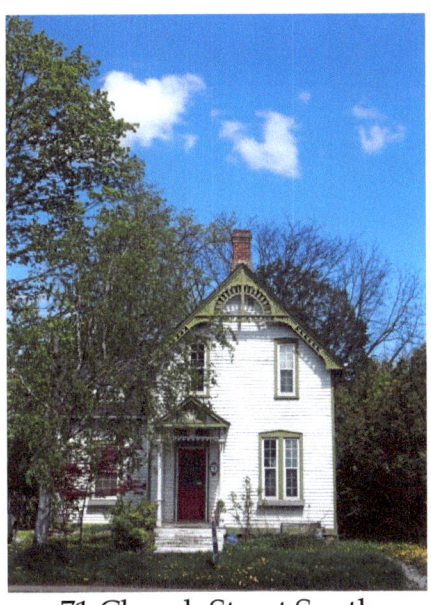

71 Church Street South

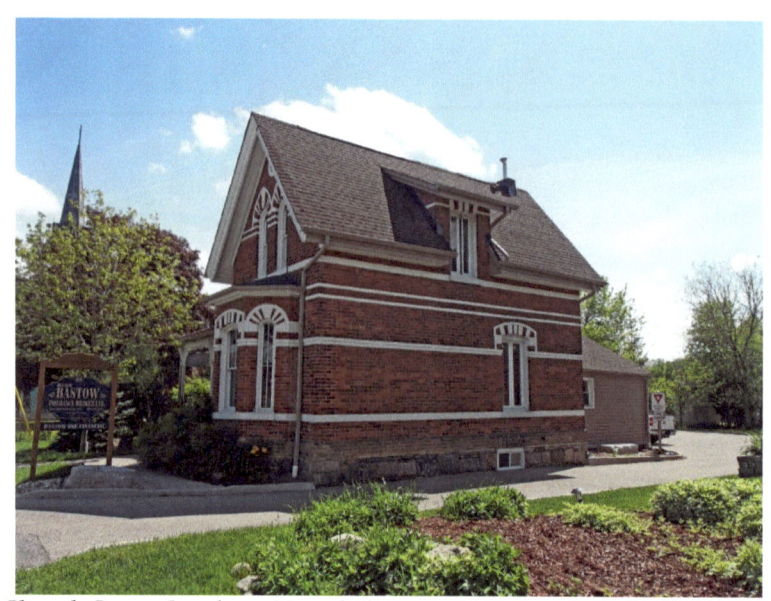

68 Church Street South – 1880 - dichromatic Italianate window treatment, gingerbread trim and brackets - Brereton Bunting, who owned this house in 1882, opened a general store along Old Kingston Road in Pickering Village in 1857 which he ran for more than 30 years. After retiring as a merchant, Mr. Bunting became a lay preacher who also served as Justice of the Peace and Postmaster. The house remained in the Bunting family from 1882 to 1946.

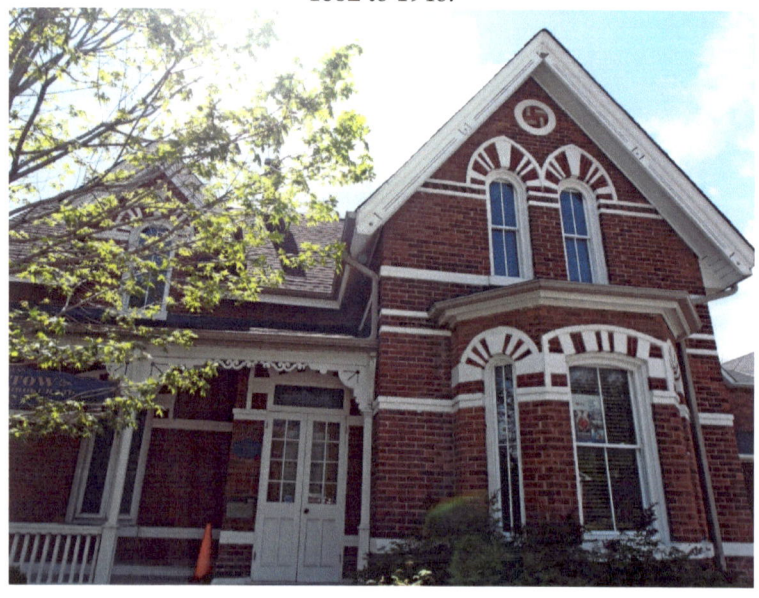

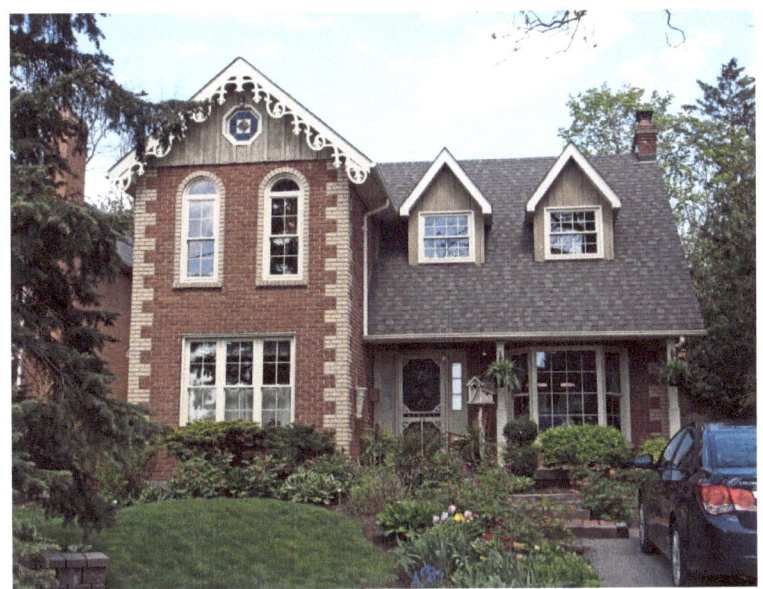

75 Church Street South – verge board trim, corner quoins

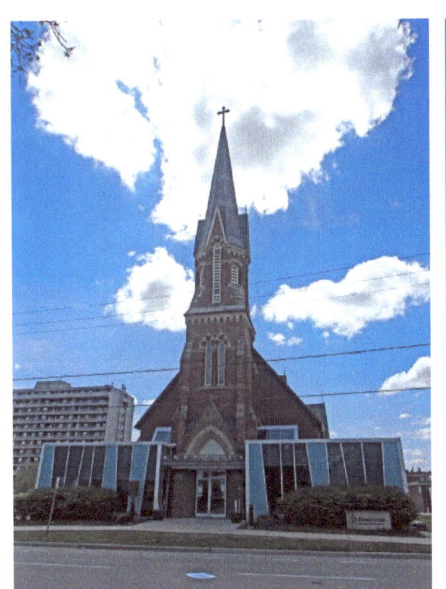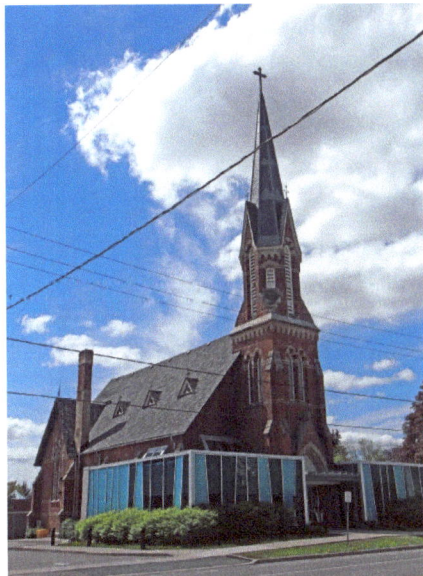

78 Church Street South

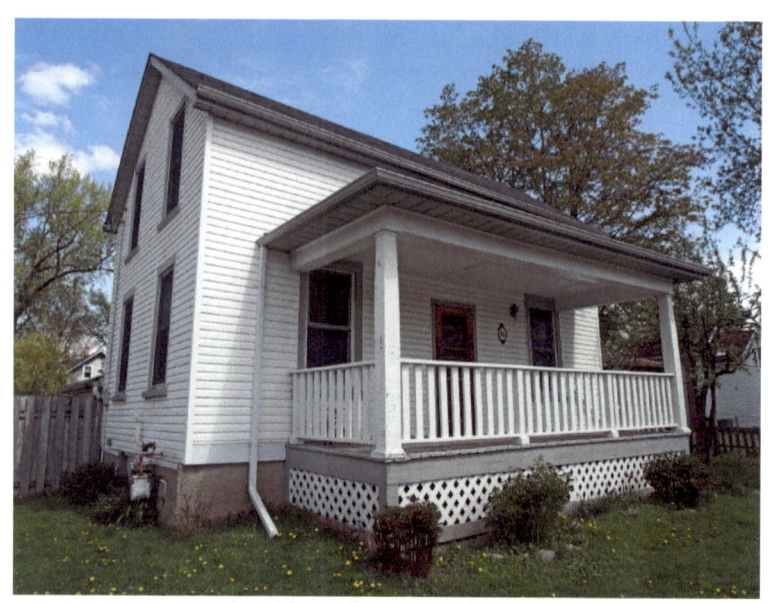
81 Church Street South

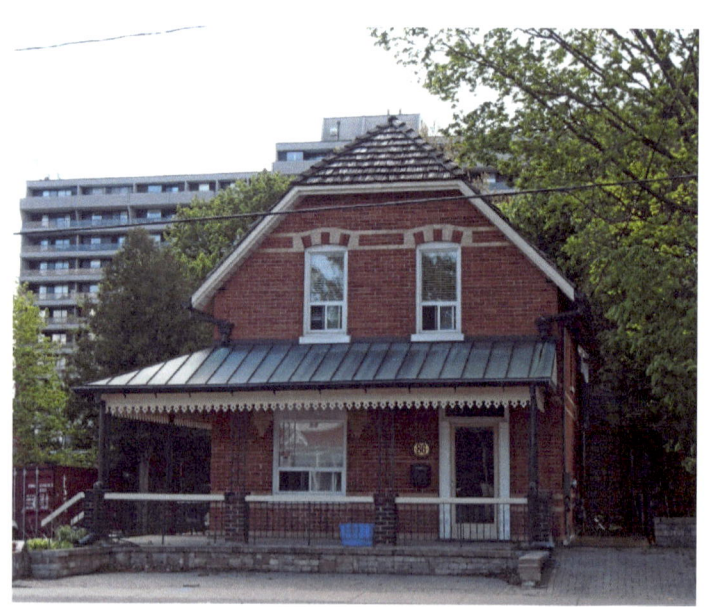
86 Church Street South

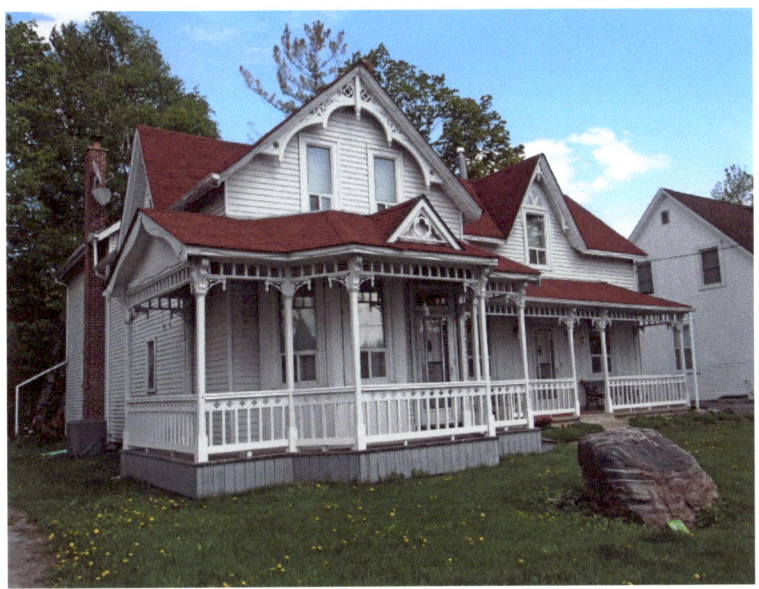

87 Church Street South

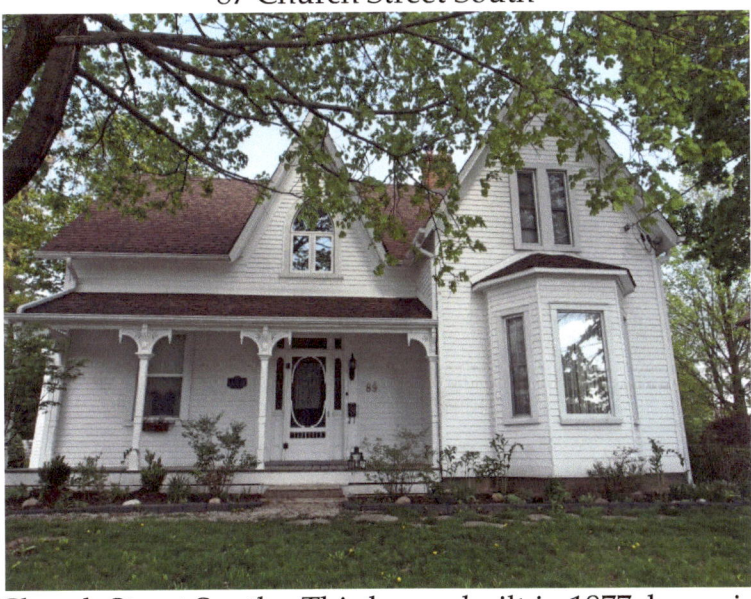

89 Church Street South - This home, built in 1877, has existed in its present configuration since 1937. It is the best preserved frame house of Gothic Revival design within the Town of Ajax.

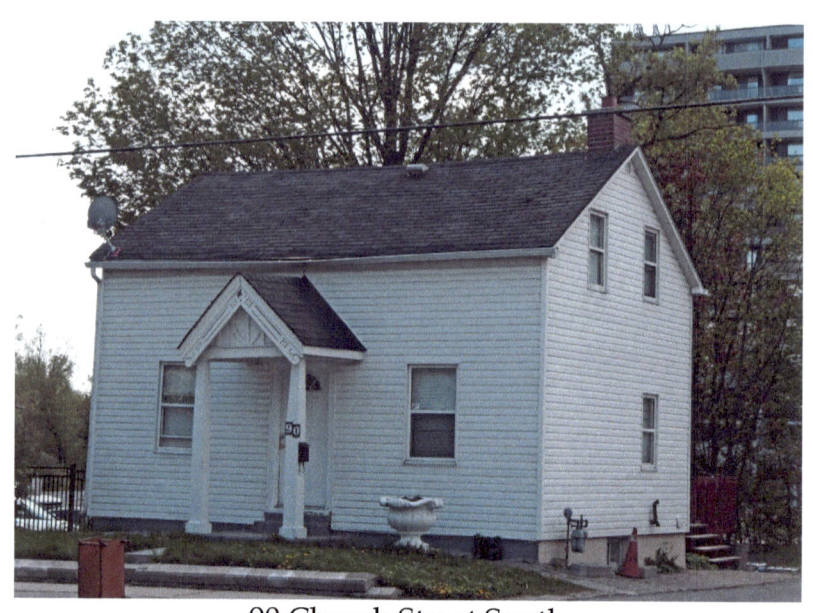

90 Church Street South

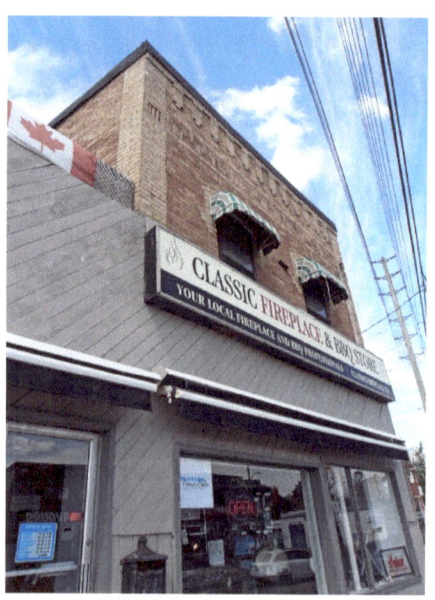

2 Old Kingston Road

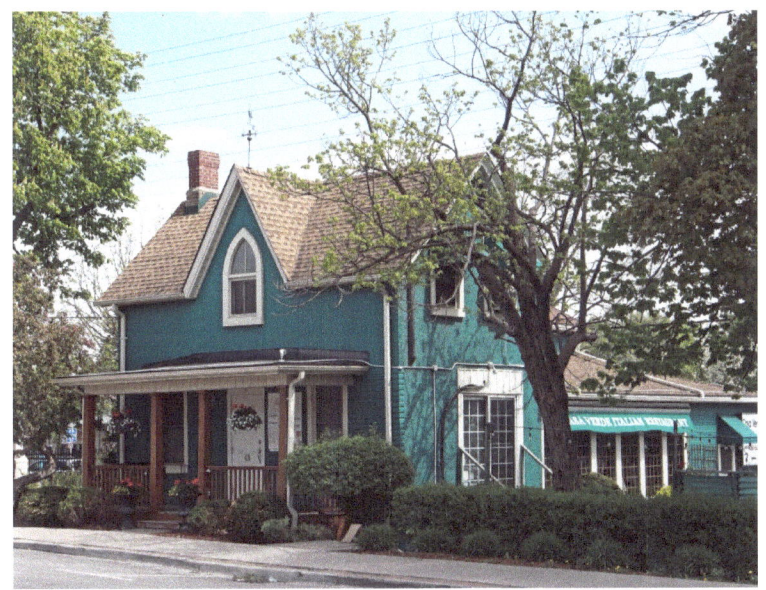

49 Old Kingston Road - Gothic

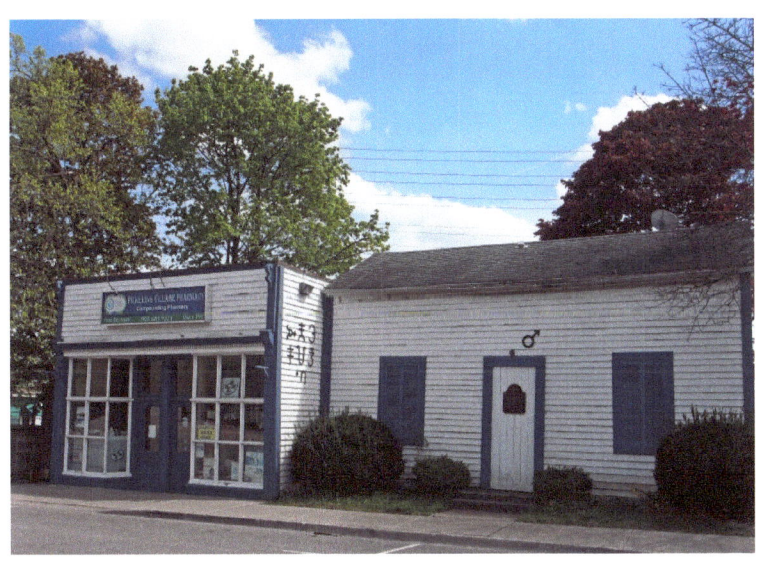

59 Old Kingston Road

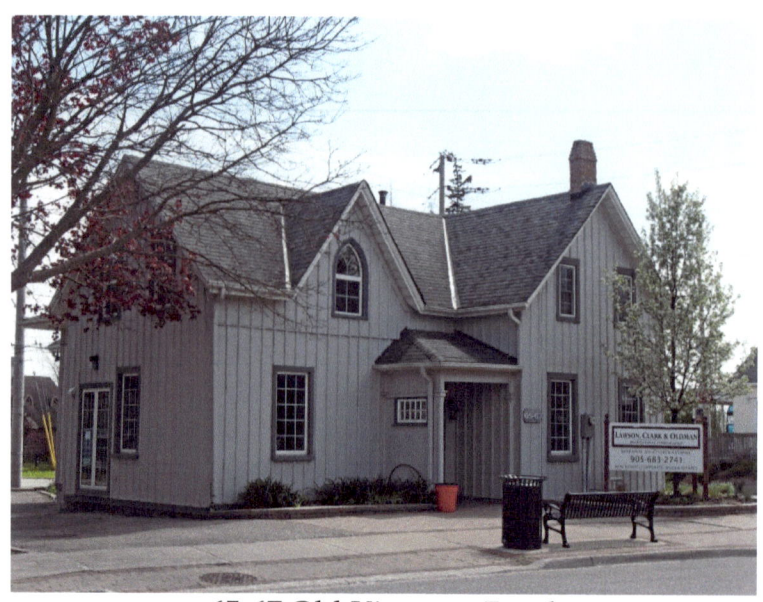

65-67 Old Kingston Road

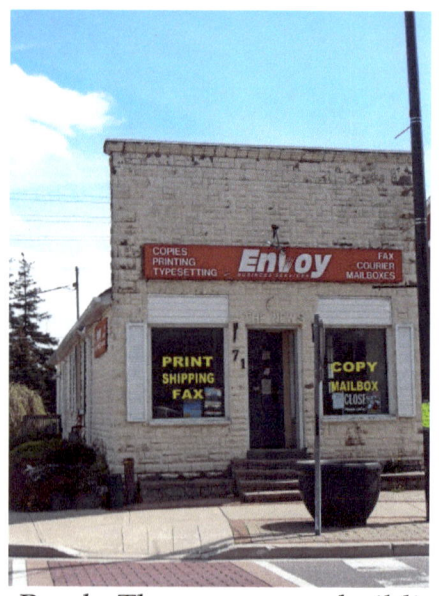

71 Old Kingston Road - The newspaper building still stands with the inscription "THE NEWS" over the front and side doors.

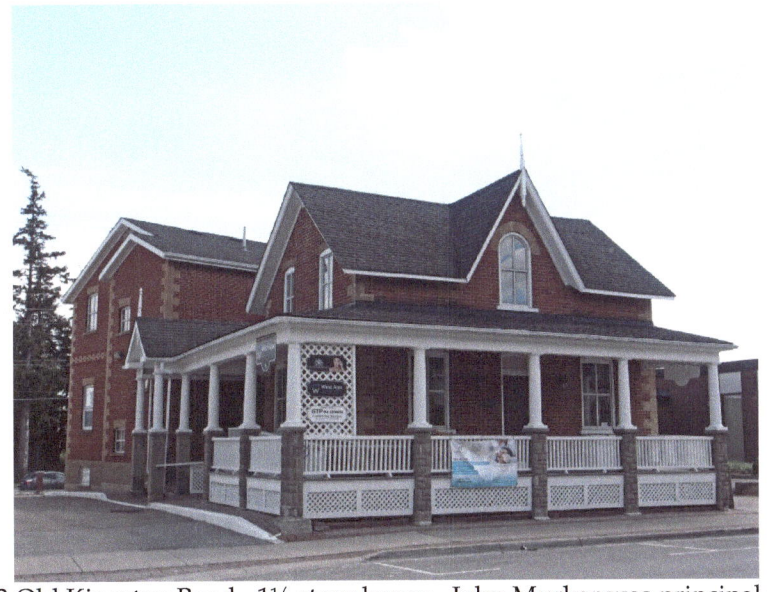

73 Old Kingston Road - 1½ story house - John Murkar was principal of Pickering Secondary School No. 4 for a period of time, after which he acquired an interest in the Pickering News. In 1907, he became the owner and publisher of the paper. After buying the house in 1912, he moved the newspaper office to the building directly east of his home.

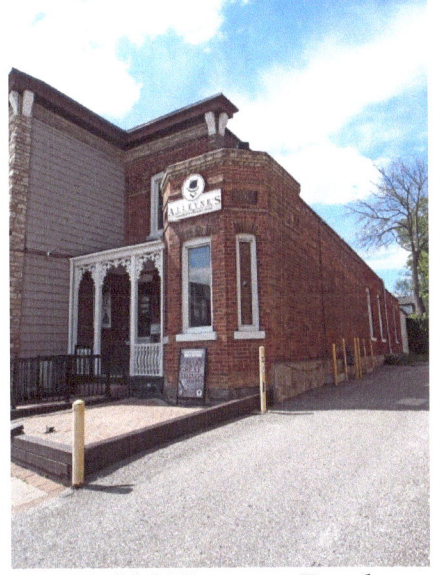

80 Old Kingston Road

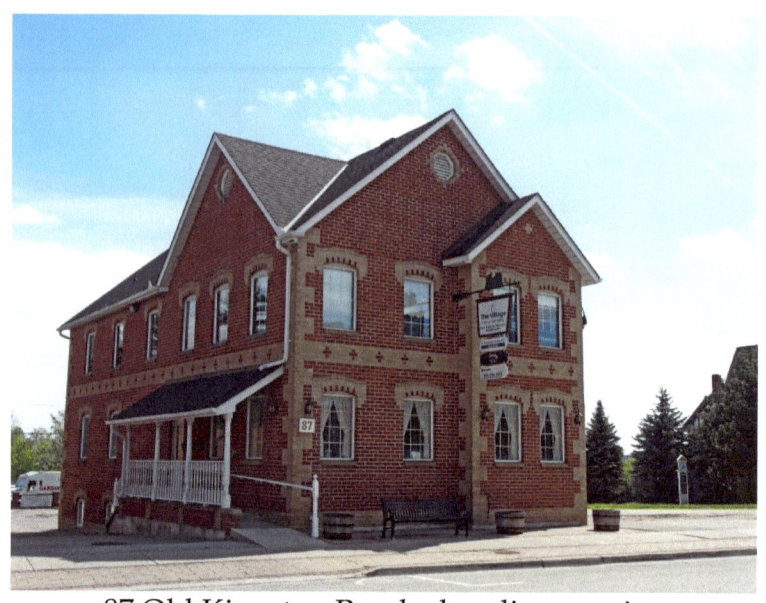

87 Old Kingston Road – banding, quoins

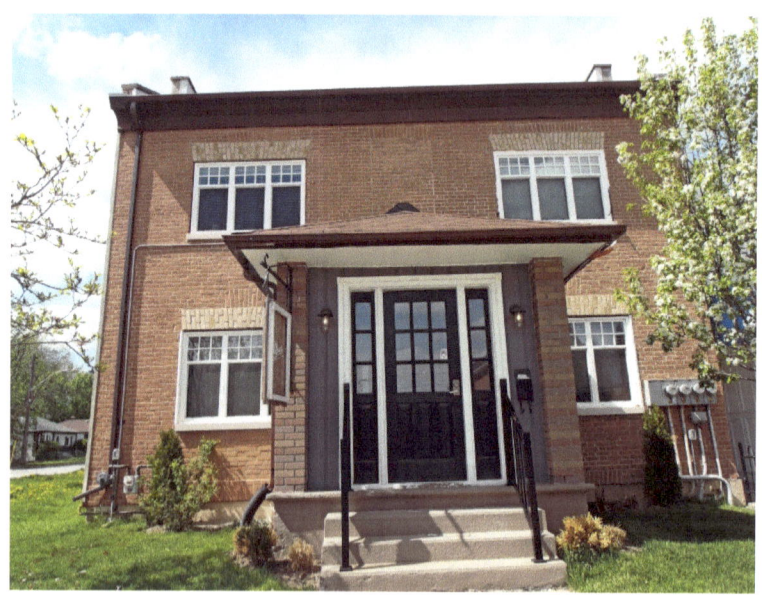

Old Kingston Road

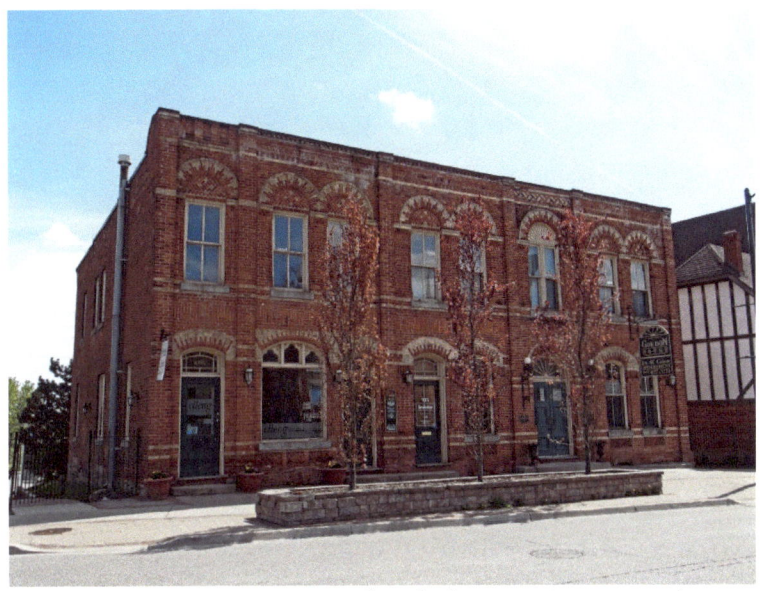

103 Old Kingston Road – dichromatic voussoirs

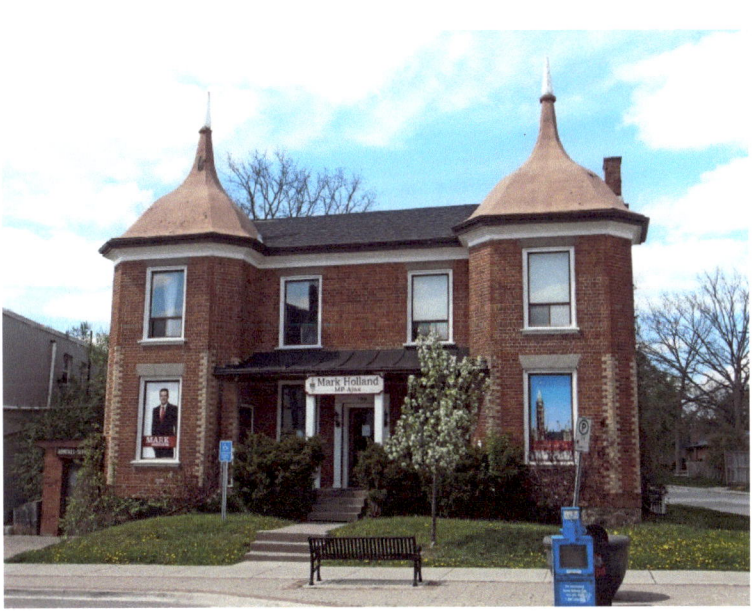

100 Old Kingston Road

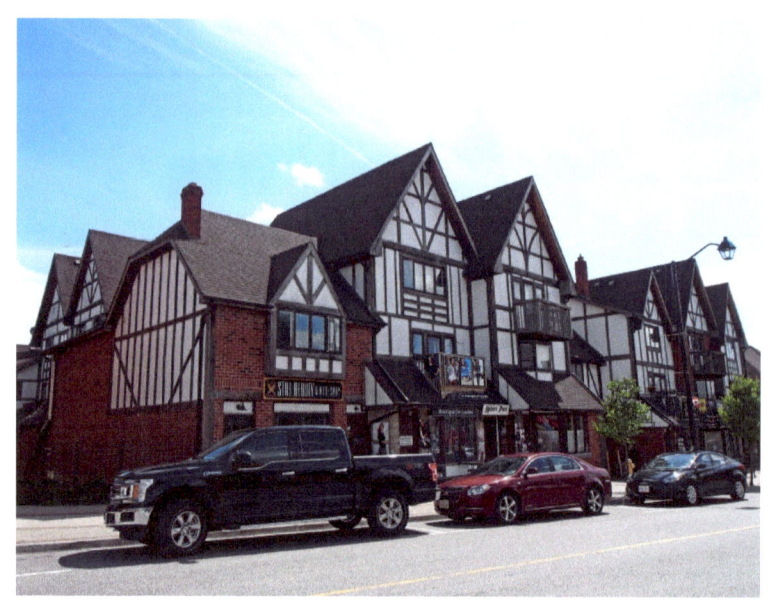

109 Old Kingston Road

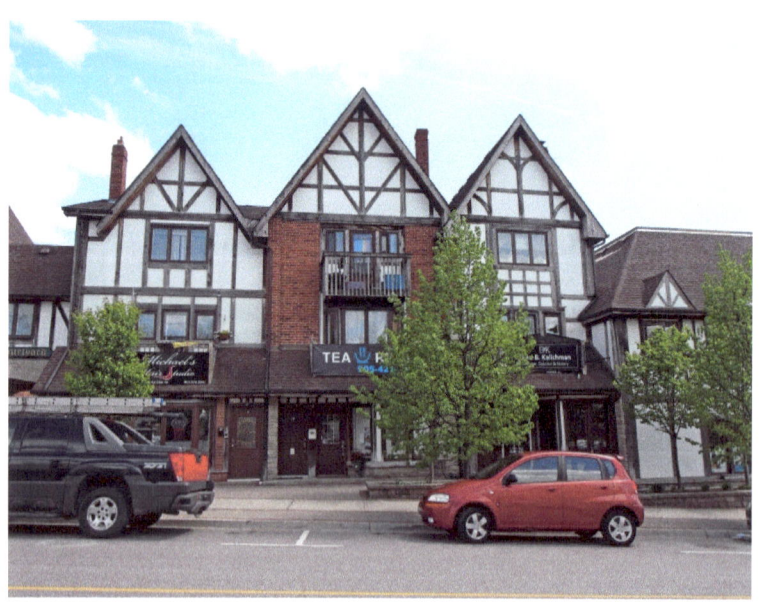

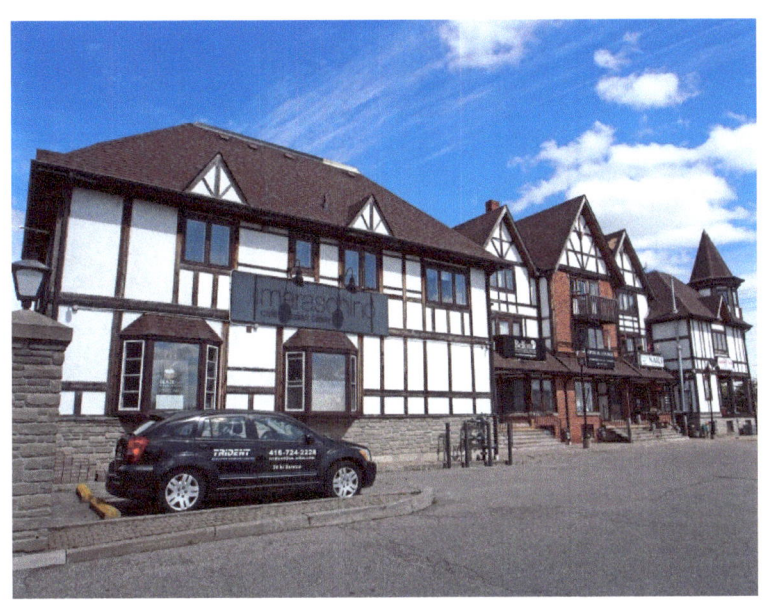

109 Old Kingston Road - Tudor

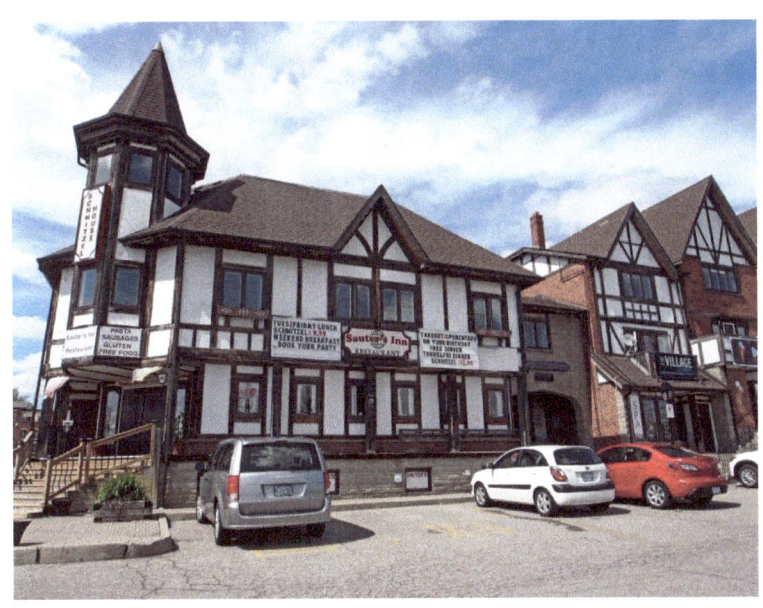

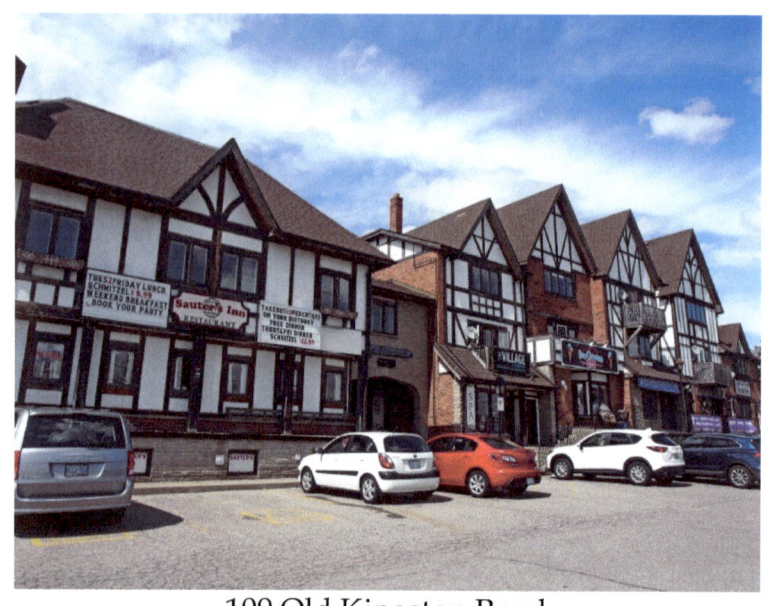

109 Old Kingston Road

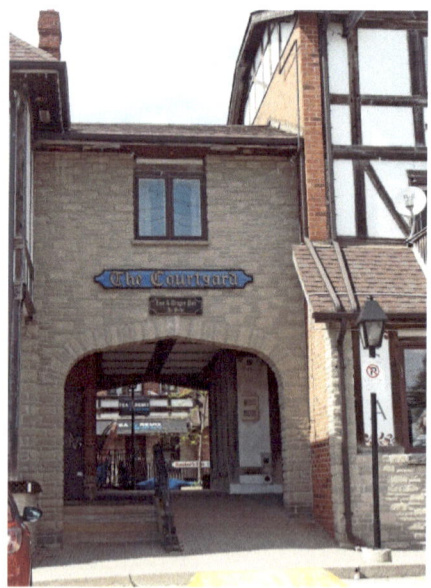

Porte-cochère

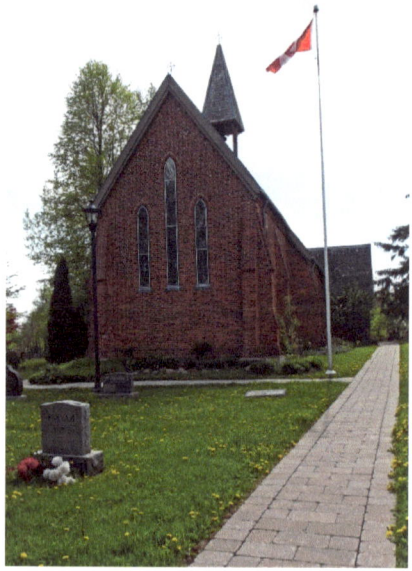

Randall Street

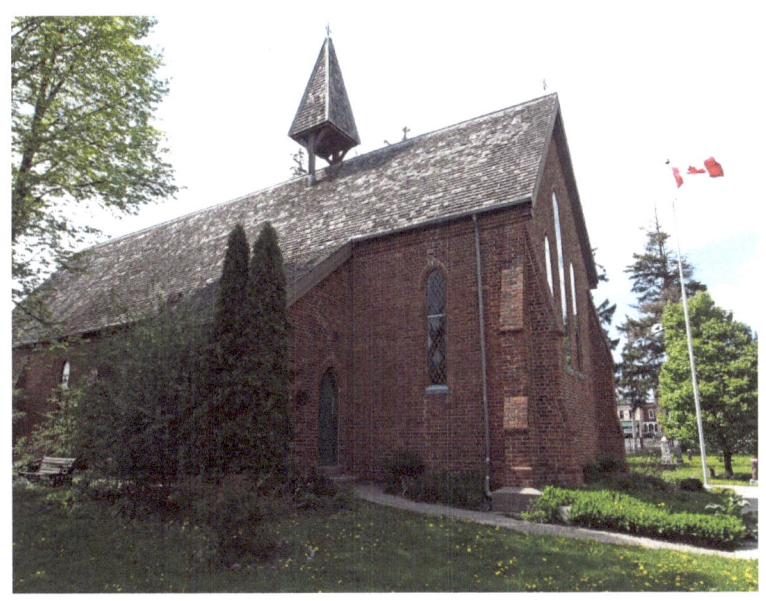

Randall Street – St. George's Anglican Church

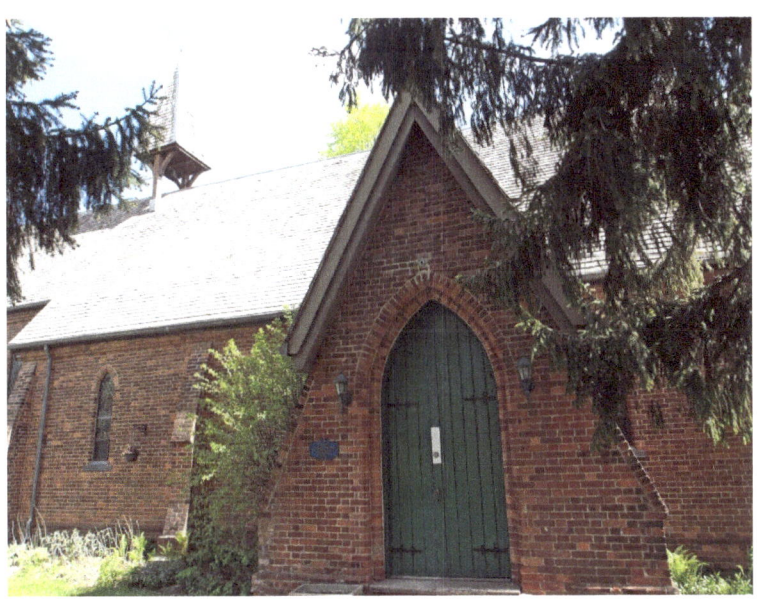

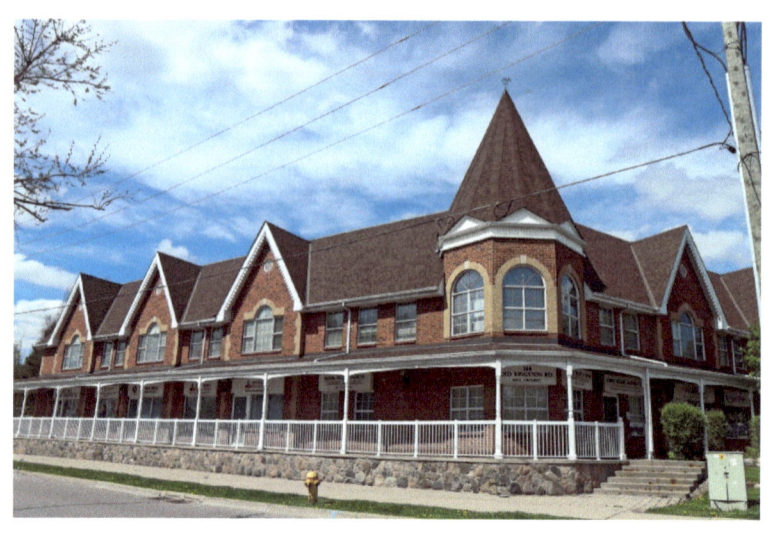

144 Old Kingston Road – corner turret

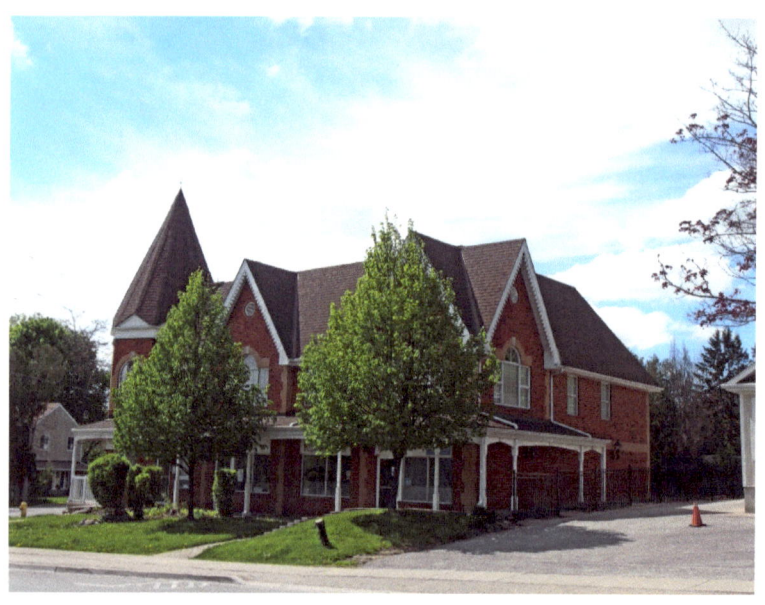

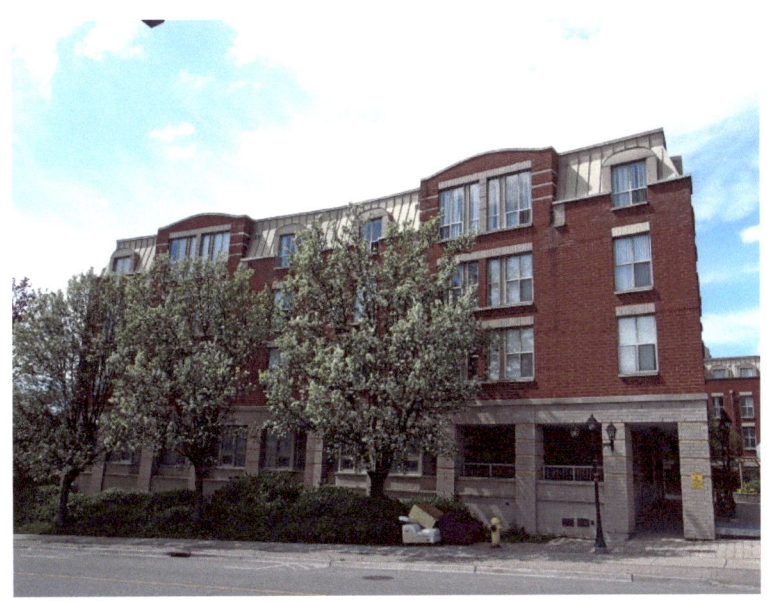

Old Kingston Road

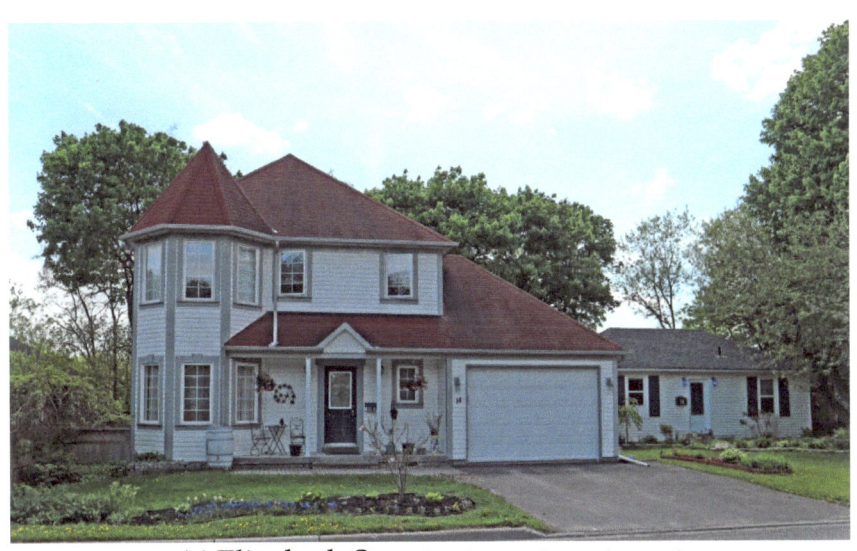

14 Elizabeth Street – two-story turret

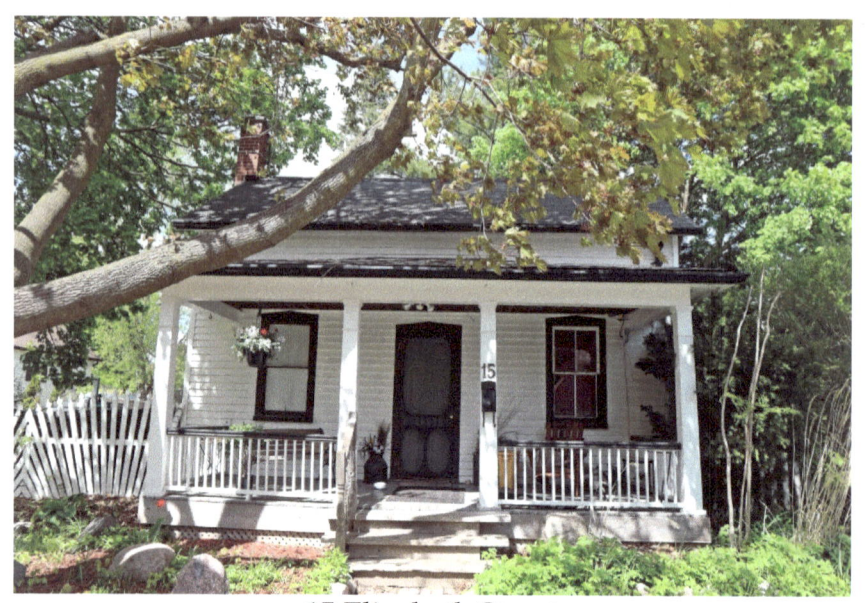
15 Elizabeth Street

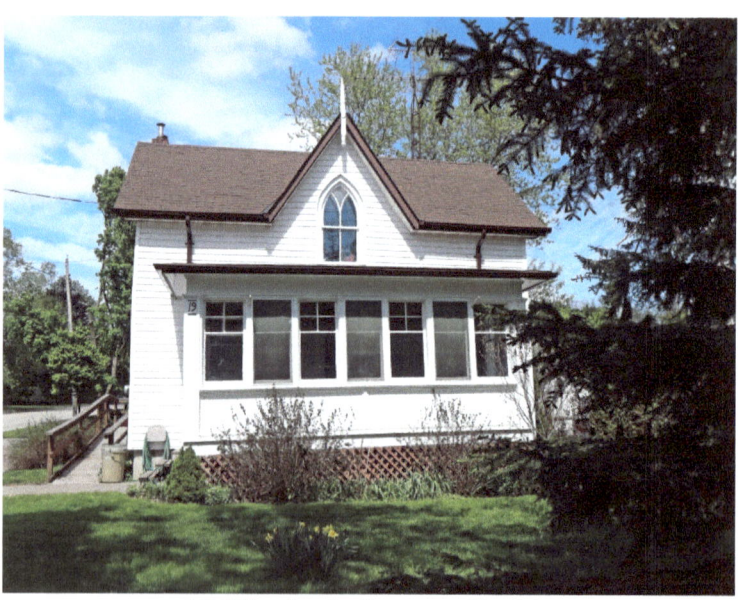
19 Elizabeth Street - Gothic

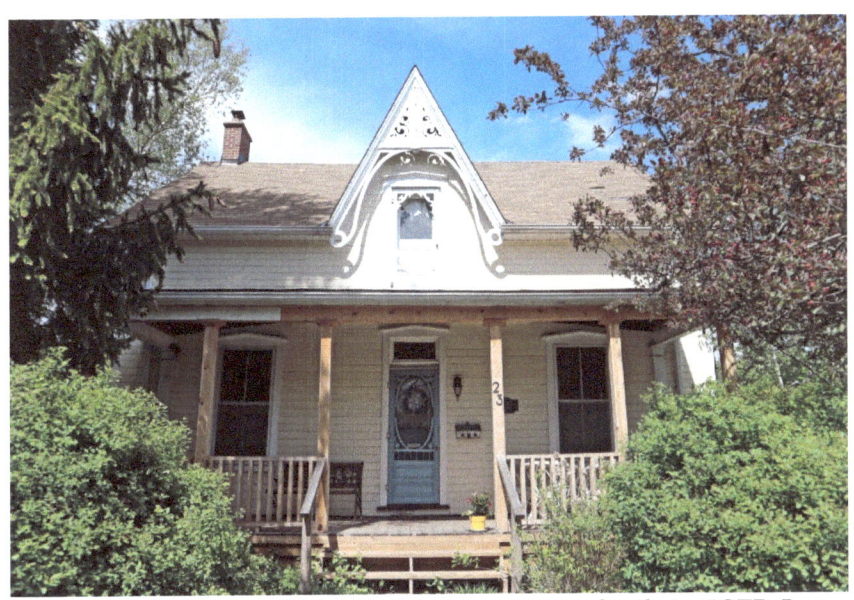

23 Elizabeth Street - This Gothic house was built in 1875. In 1980 the owners restored the tongue and grove pine wood facade. Other features include the decorative trim above the front gable and a second story "suicide" door. Tradition says is was the first house equipped with inside plumbing and central heating - features installed to persuade a retired miller from Toronto to run the Spink's Mill on nearby Duffin's Creek during World War I.

Pickering

Pickering is home to the Pickering Nuclear Generating Station, an eight-reactor facility with a capacity of 4,120 megawatts.

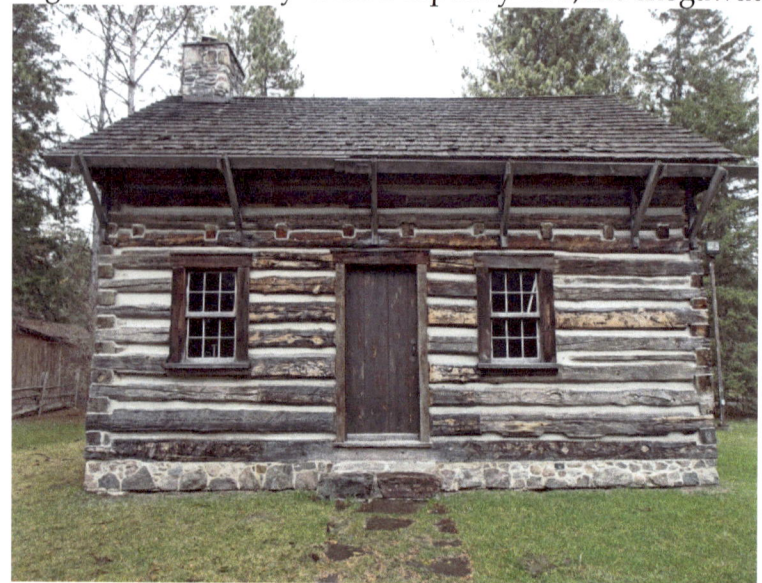

2365 Concession Rd 6, Greenwood - Log cabin at Pickering Museum Village

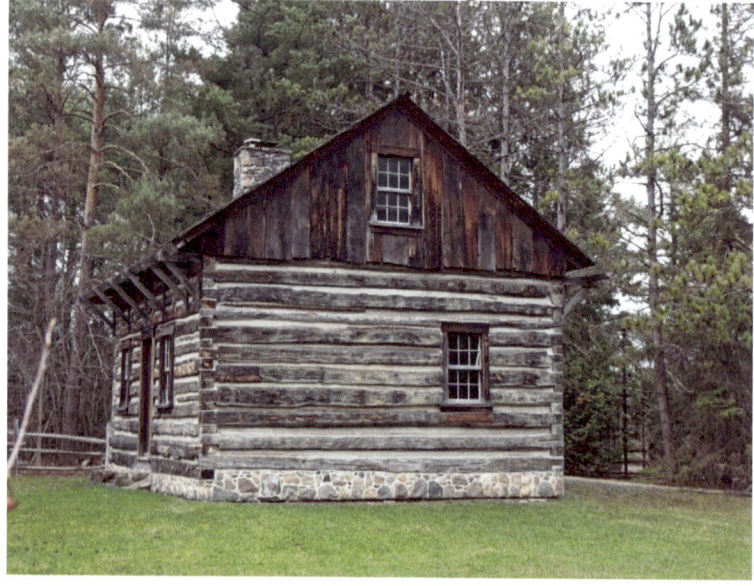

Hamlet of Brougham

Brougham is a community within the northern part of the City of Pickering. Some of its lands are affected by plans to build the proposed Pickering Airport. There are concerns because some of its buildings are of architectural significance

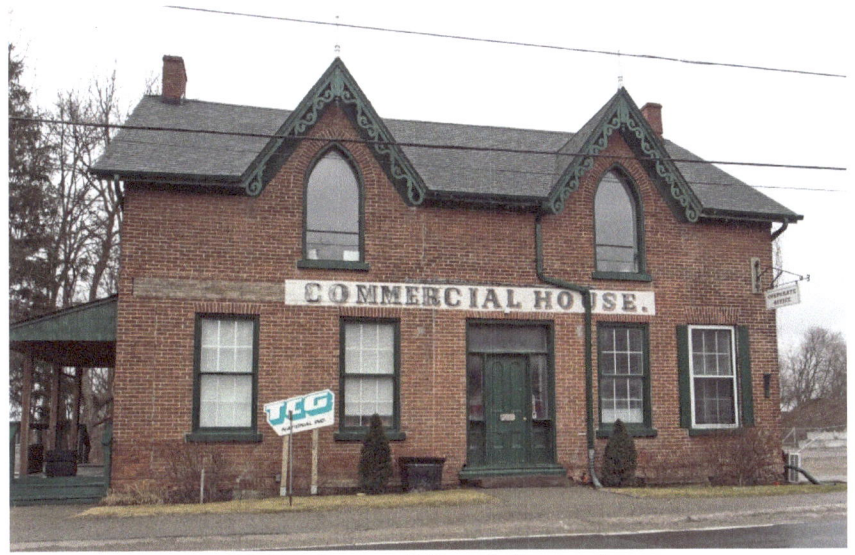

1709 Highway 7 Road, Brougham

The Former Commercial Hotel in Brougham, Ontario is a two-story brick building in the Gothic Revival style with a gable roof and has pointed arched windows in two dormers with finials and decorative wood fascia. It was initially built as a home and then converted into a hotel.

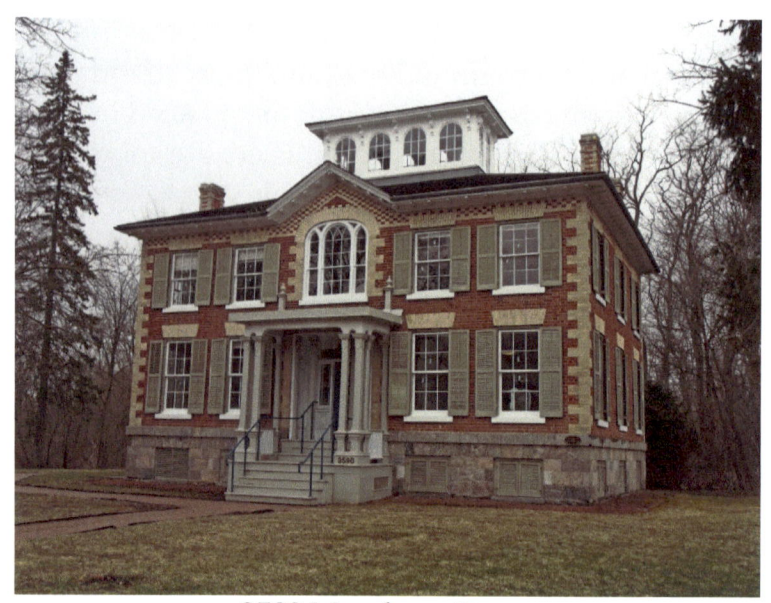

3590 Mowbray Street

Bentley House was built in 1853-55 for William Bentley, a local businessman and founder of Brougham village. It remained in the Bentley family until 1959, when it was purchased and restored by the Gibson family. The site is now part of the proposed Pickering Airport. Bentley House, on its original four-acre site, is located at the intersection of the Brock Road and Highway 7.

The Italianate style has two variations. The Tuscan Villa style reflects the Picturesque values of variety in silhouette and textures and intricacy in detail, while the Italian Palazzo form emphasizes the symmetry and tripartite composition typical of Renaissance buildings. The heritage character of Bentley House resides in its vernacular Italianate style, as evidenced by the combination of Renaissance massing with Picturesque expression in the materials and detailing.

The Renaissance influence on the design of Bentley House is reflected in its symmetrical massing, shallow hip roof, regular arrangement of windows on all façades, and round-headed windows in the belvedere. Picturesque qualities are expressed in the variety of colors and textures of materials: stone foundation, polychrome red-and-buff brickwork, large multi-paned sash windows, and elaborate wood trim and wood belvedere. The emphasis on ornamentation typical of Italianate villas in the Picturesque tradition is reflected in the tracery of the segmentally-arched window in the gable, eave brackets and dentils on both the house and belvedere, paneled door casing with carved colonnettes in antis, carved porch pillars, window shutters, and prominent decorative chimneys.

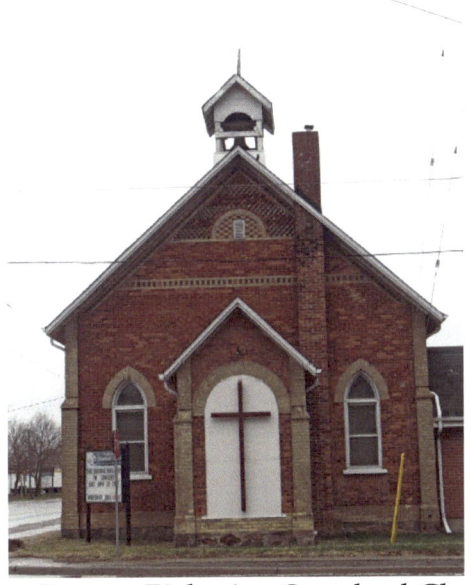

3595 Mowbray Street – Pickering Standard Church – Gothic, lancet windows, banding

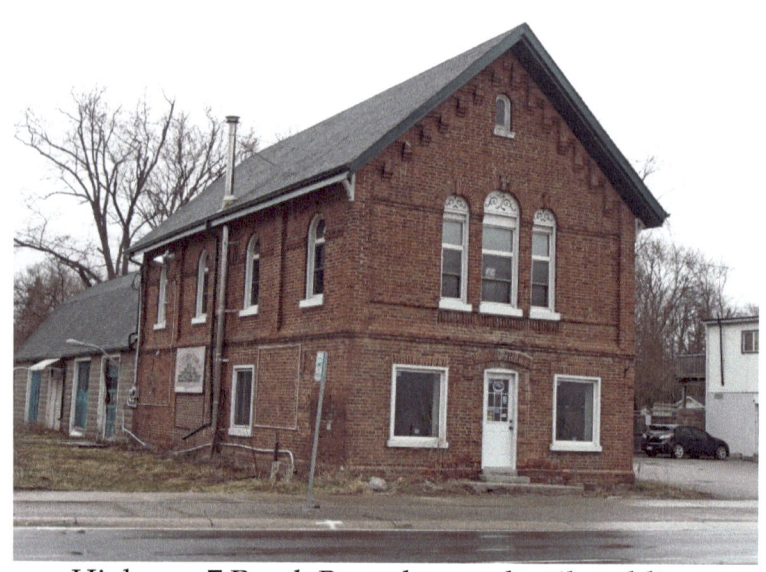
Highway 7 Road, Brougham – dentil molding

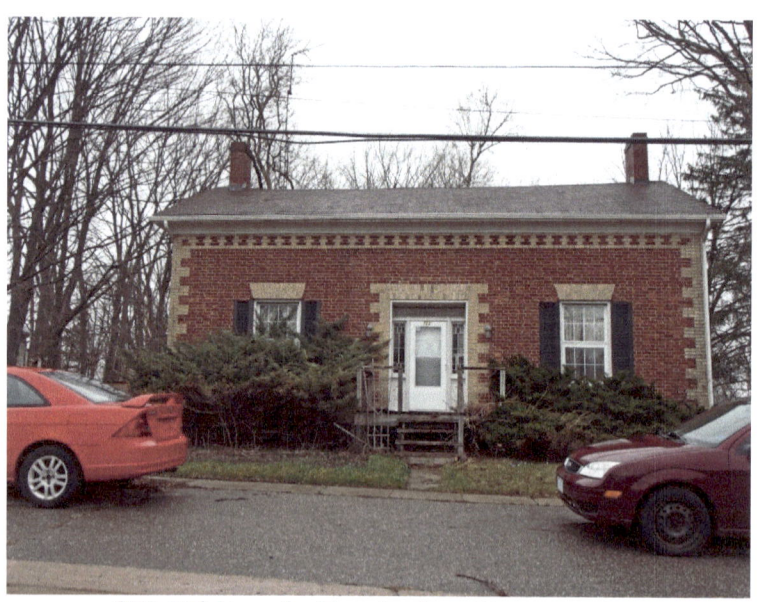
353 Whitevale Road – banding, quoins

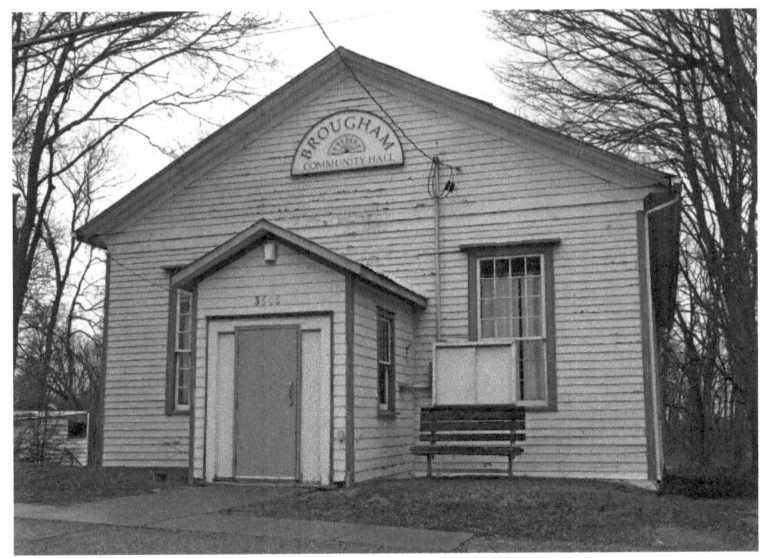

3545 Brock Road – 1854 - The Former Pickering Township Hall is a one-story wood frame structure on a stone foundation, with a gable roof, a symmetrical façade and large paned windows. It is located on a narrow site facing Brock Road in the small hamlet of Brougham, Ontario.

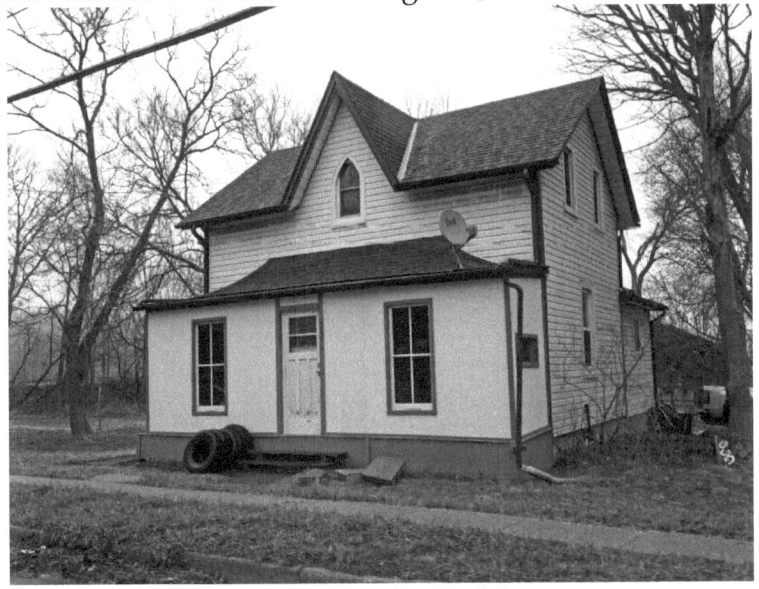

Brock Road - Gothic

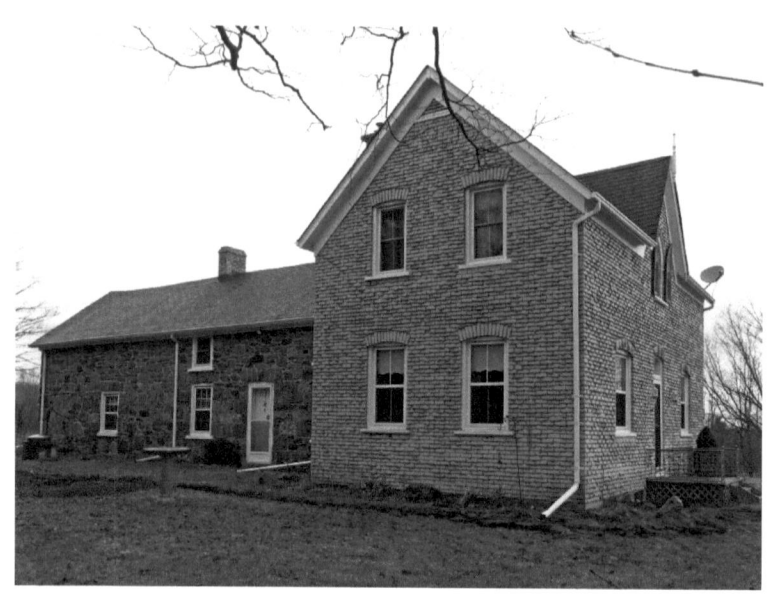

3285 Sideline 20 – coarse fieldstone house

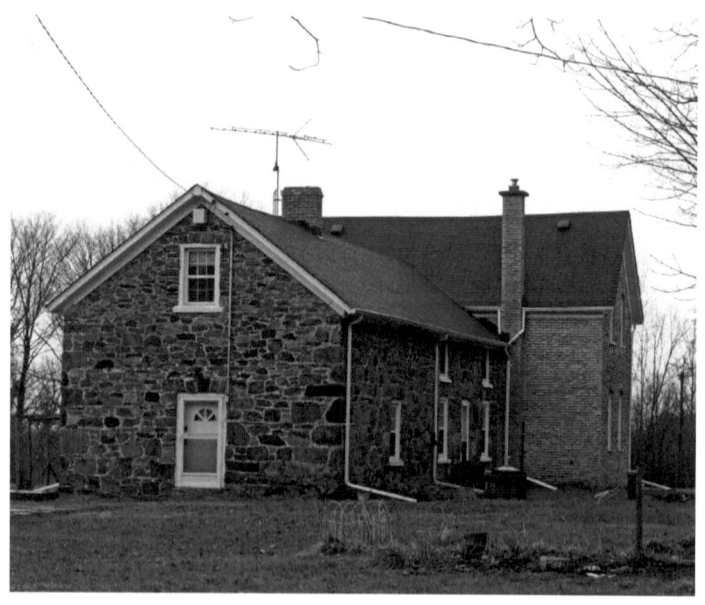

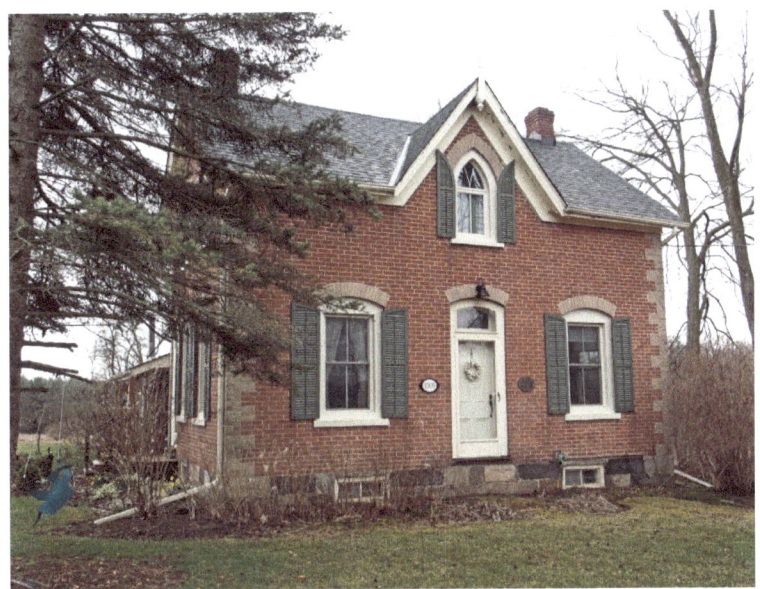

1505 Whitevale Road – Wilson House – 1861 – Ontario vernacular farmhouse – corner quoins, finial on gable

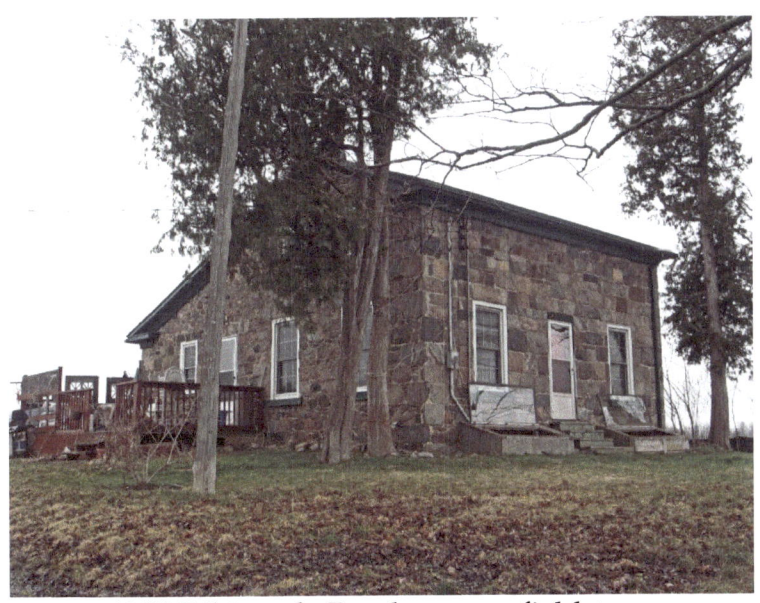

1390 Whitevale Road - coarse fieldstone

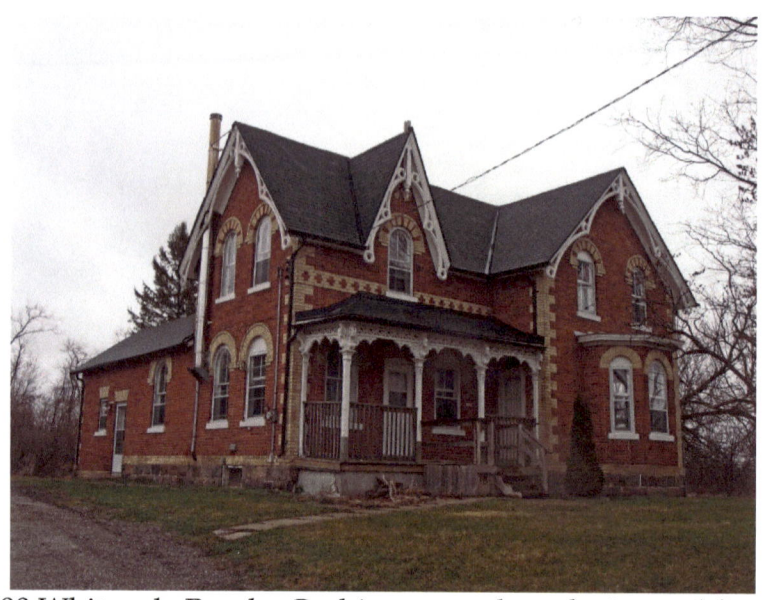

1200 Whitevale Road – Gothic – verge board trim and finials on gables, banding, corner quoins, bay window

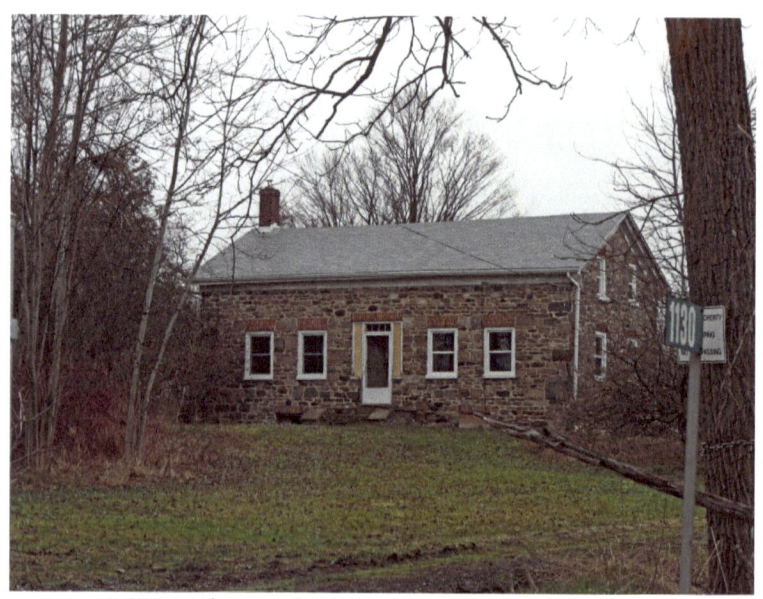

1130 Whitevale Road - coarse fieldstone

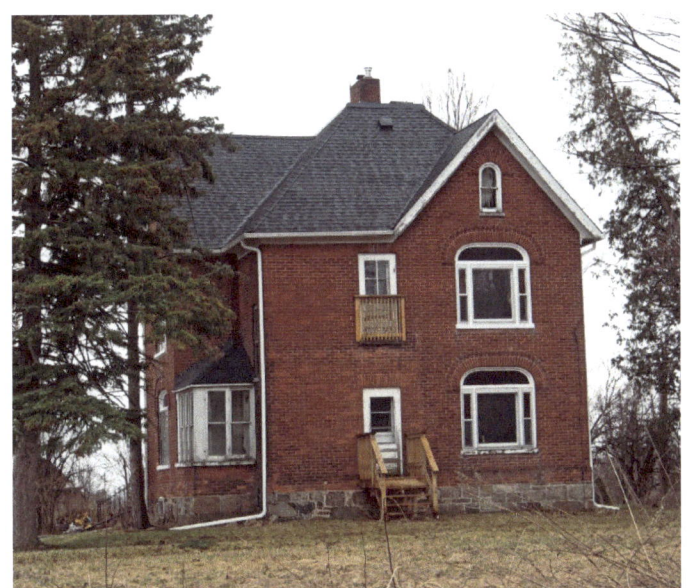

1125 Whitevale Road

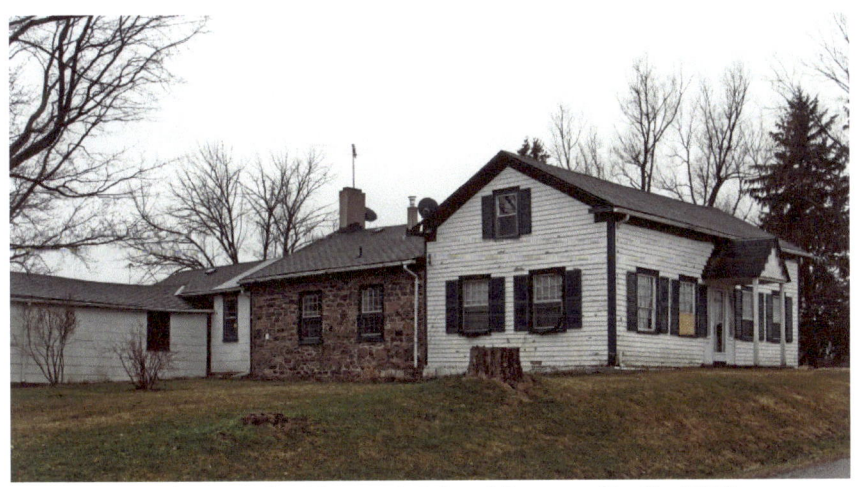

615 Whitevale Road - Henry Major House - Built 1820s - Farmstead, one story frame house, stone kitchen addition built between 1851 and 1861

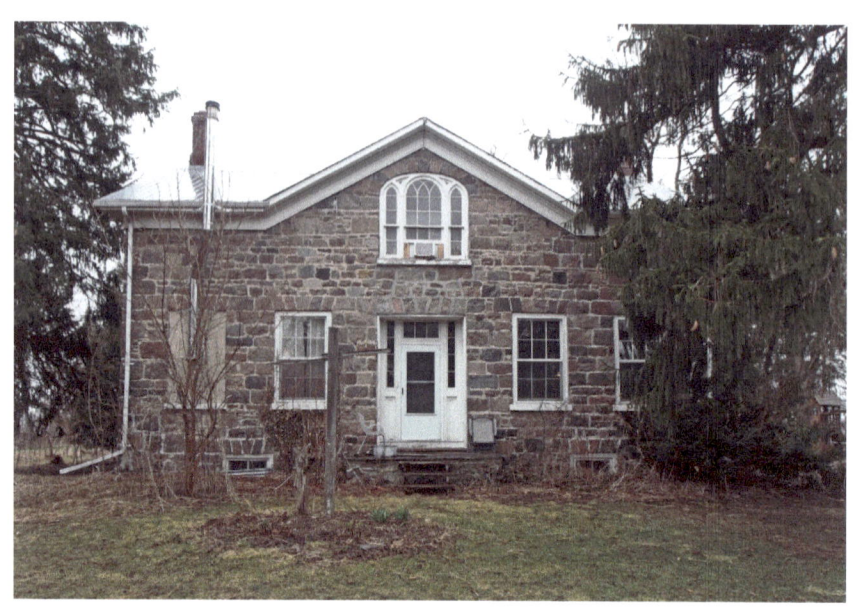

940 Whitevale Road - - John Major House - Built 1822 - Farmstead, coarse fieldstone, 1½ story house with a summer kitchen addition and one-story stone woodshed

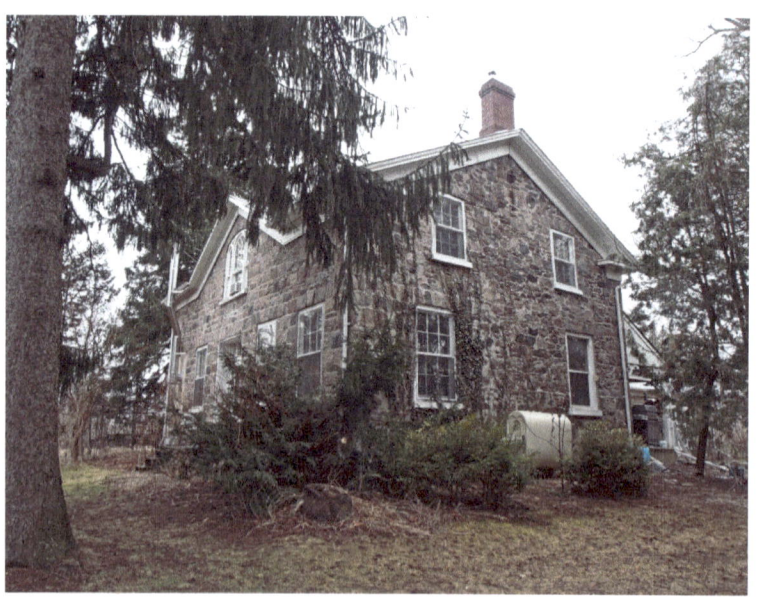

Hamlet of Whitevale

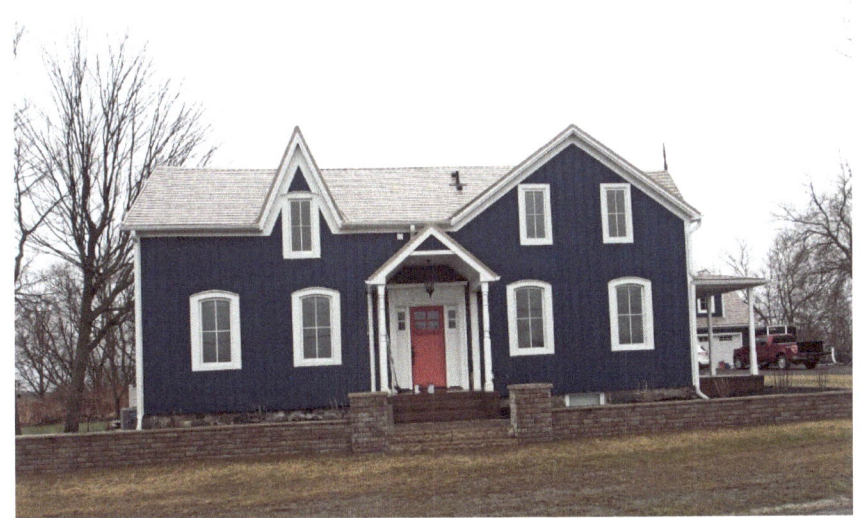

565 Whitevale Road

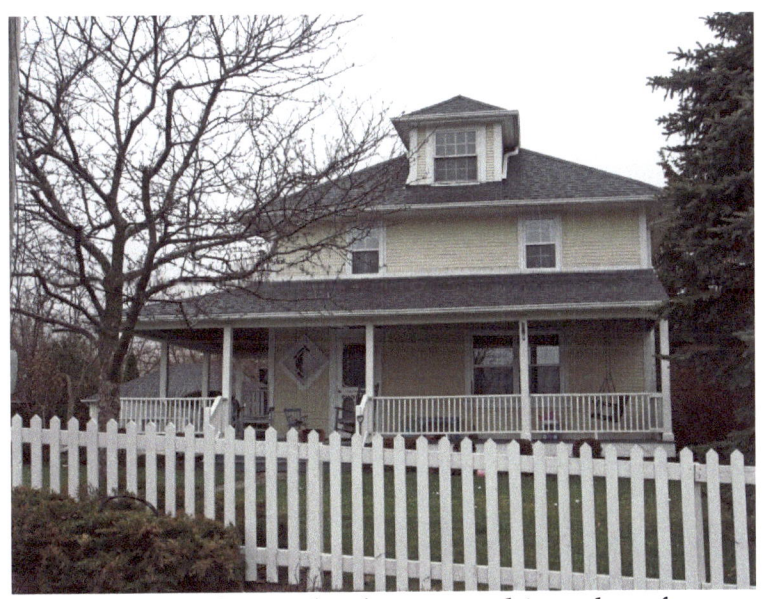

Whitevale Road – dormer on hipped roof

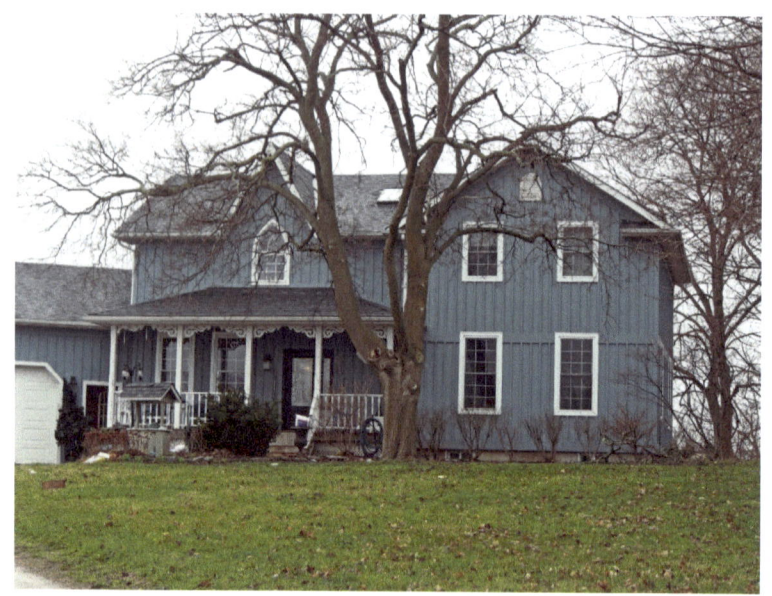

545 Whitevale Road

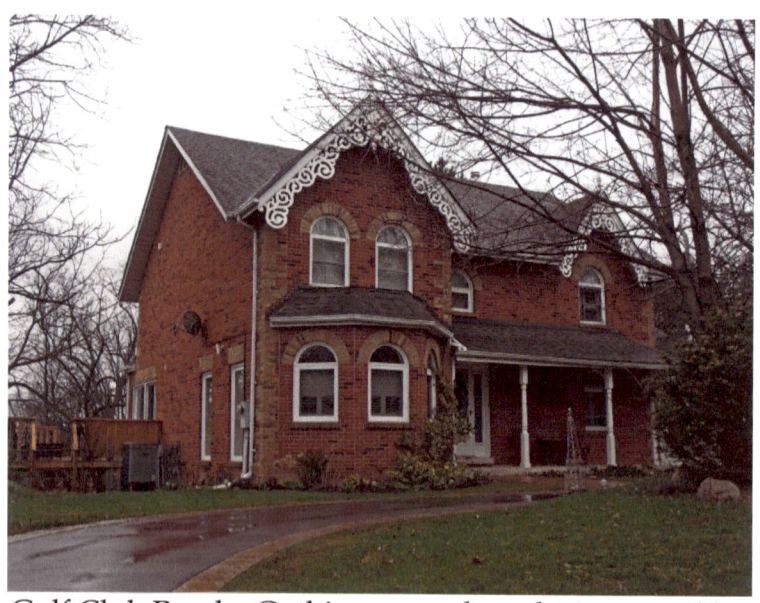

Golf Club Road – Gothic – verge board trim on gables

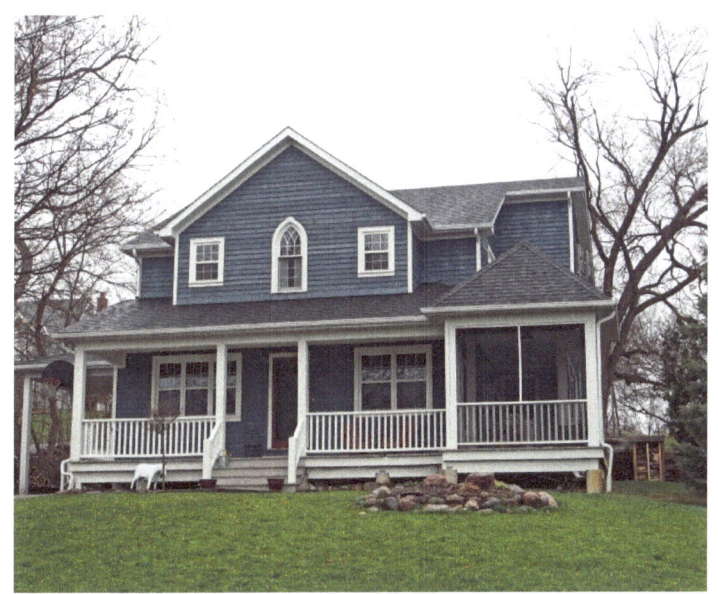

3177 Golf Club Road

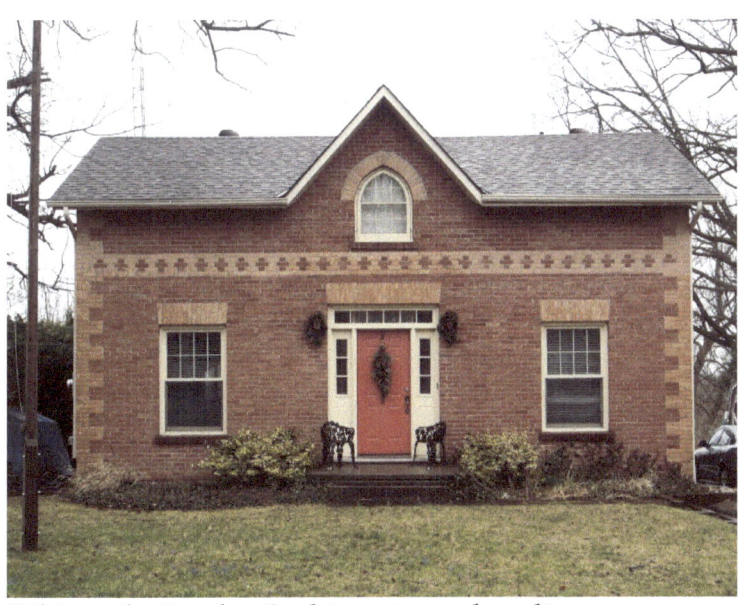

503 Whitevale Road – Gothic cottage, banding, corner quoins

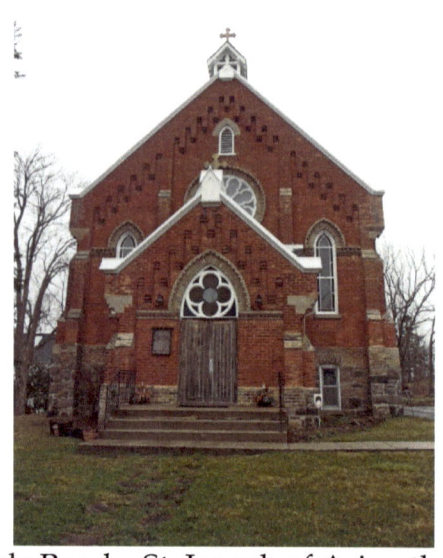

510 Whitevale Road – St. Joseph of Arimathea Orthodox Church – 1884 – originally a Methodist Church – Gothic Revival style

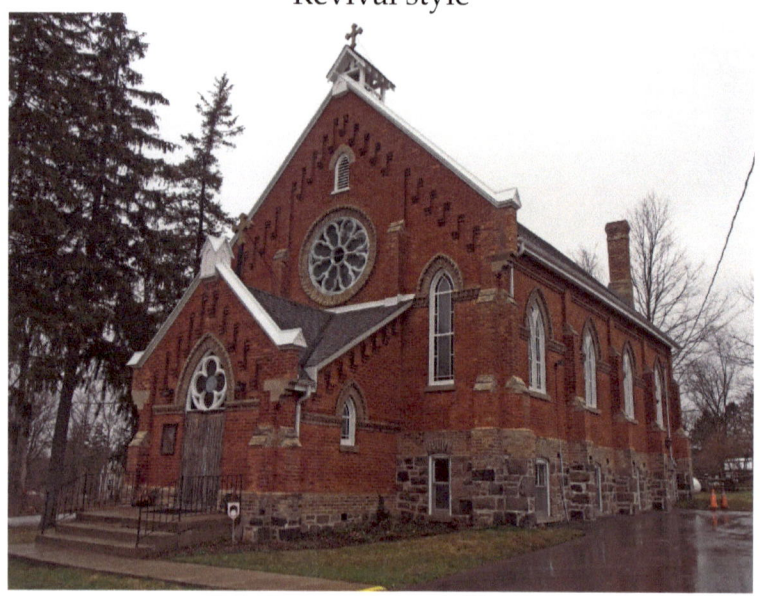

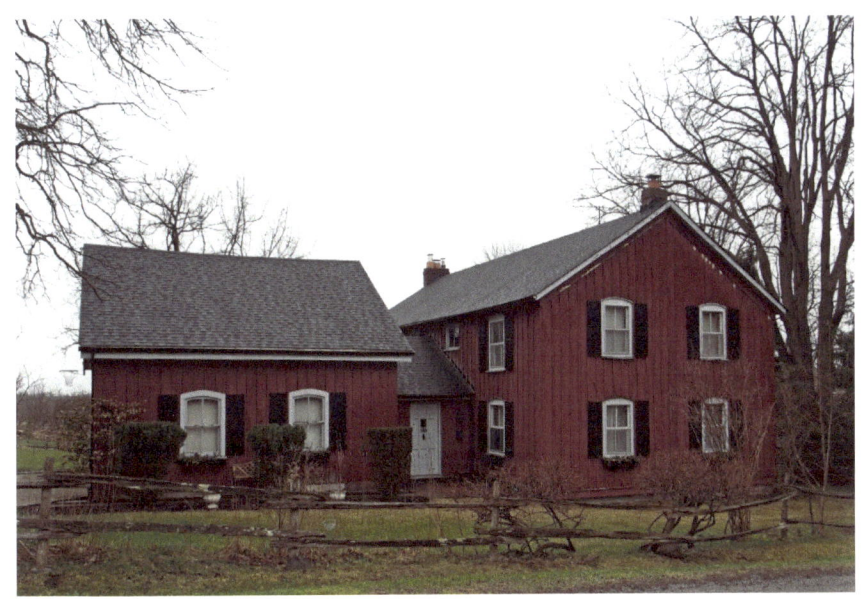

499 Whitevale Road

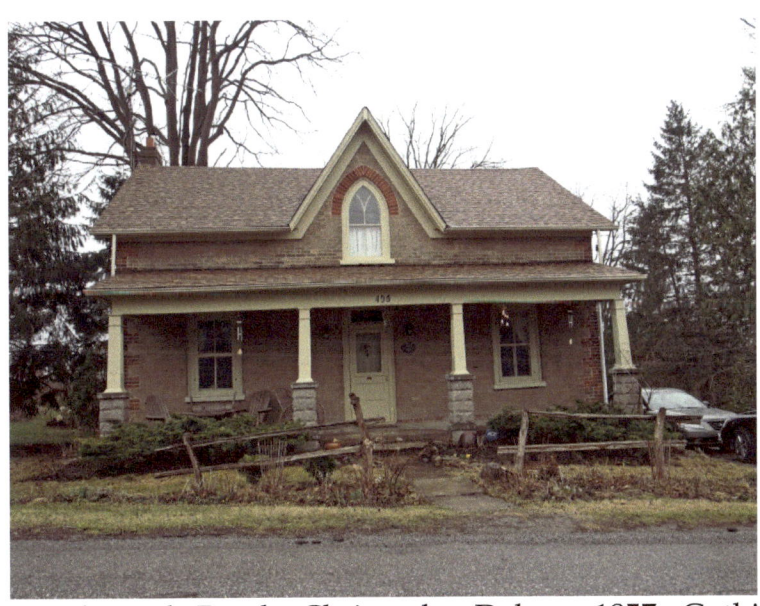

495 Whitevale Road – Christopher Dale - c. 1857 - Gothic

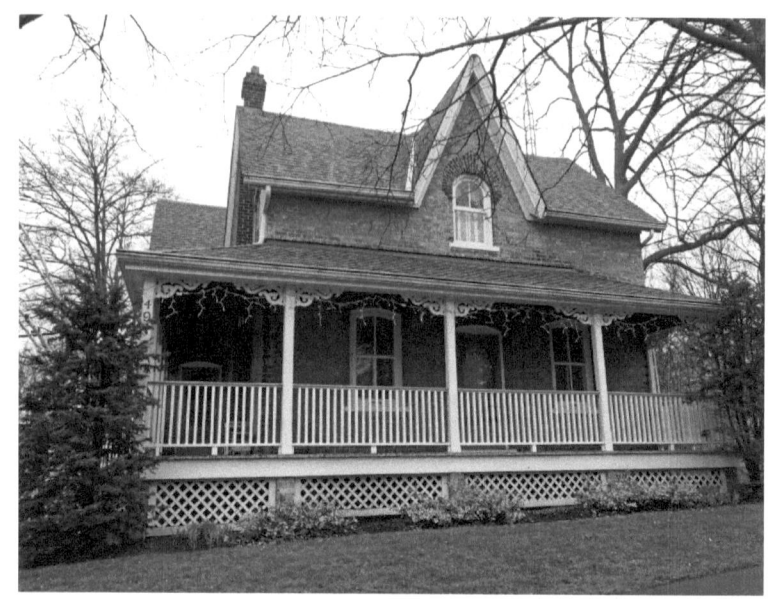

494 Whitevale Road - Gothic

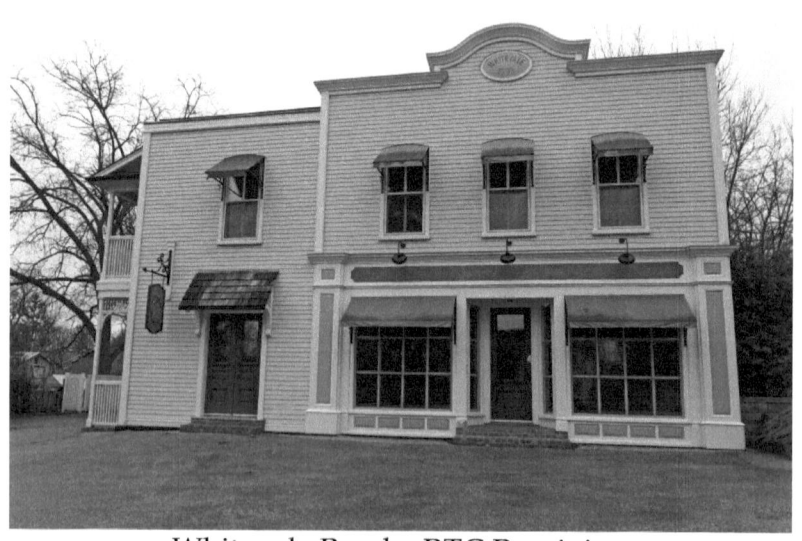

Whitevale Road – RTC Receiving

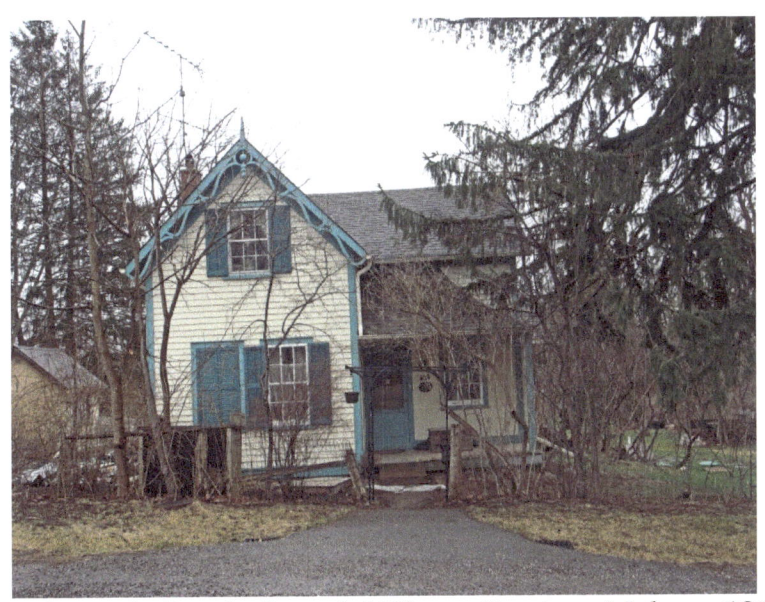

489 Whitevale Road – Joseph Wilson, Carriage Maker – 1860 – Gothic, verge board trim and finial

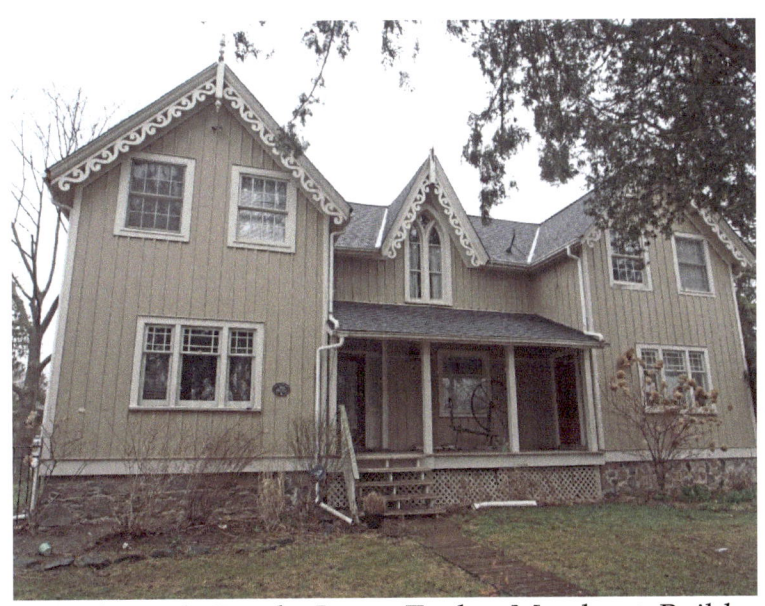

480 Whitevale Road – James Taylor, Merchant, Builder – c. 1868 – Gothic, verge board trim, finials

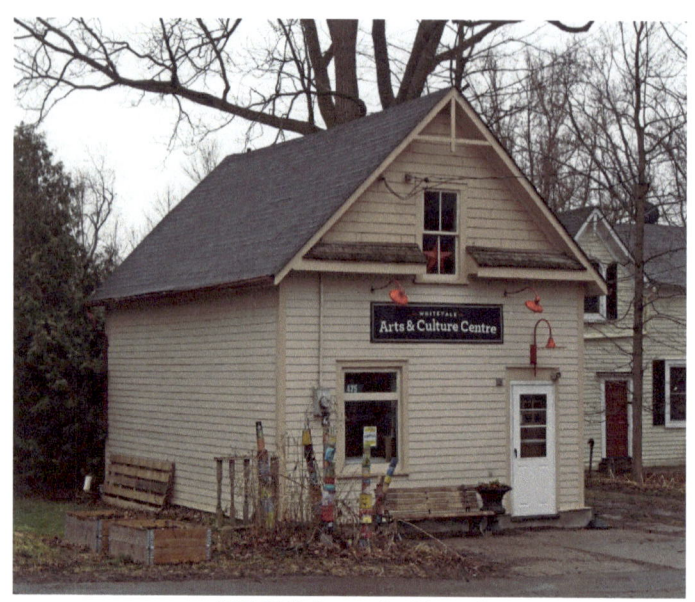

475 Whitevale Road

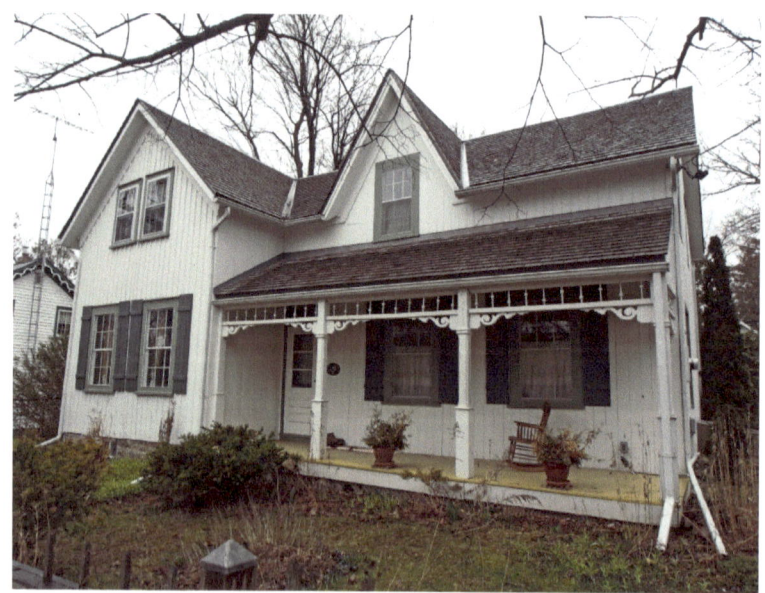

470 Whitevale Road – Daniel Moody, Shoemaker – 1860 - Gothic

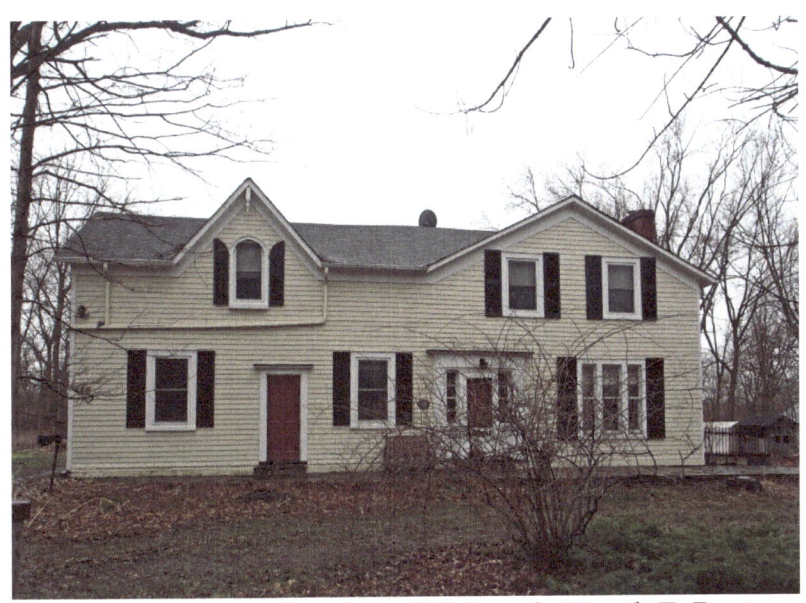

465 Whitevale Road – 1845 – Whitevale Hotel, T. Burton, Proprietor – c. 1845

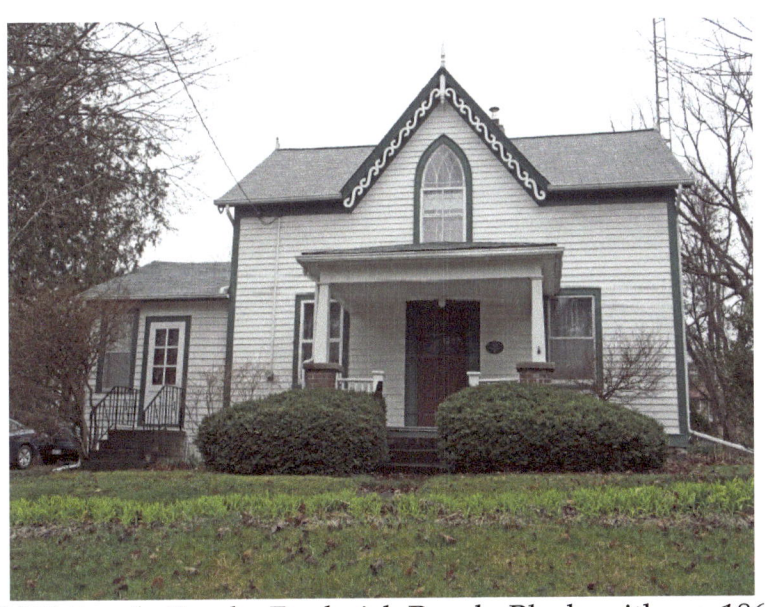

460 Whitevale Road – Frederick Roach, Blacksmith – c. 1868 - Gothic

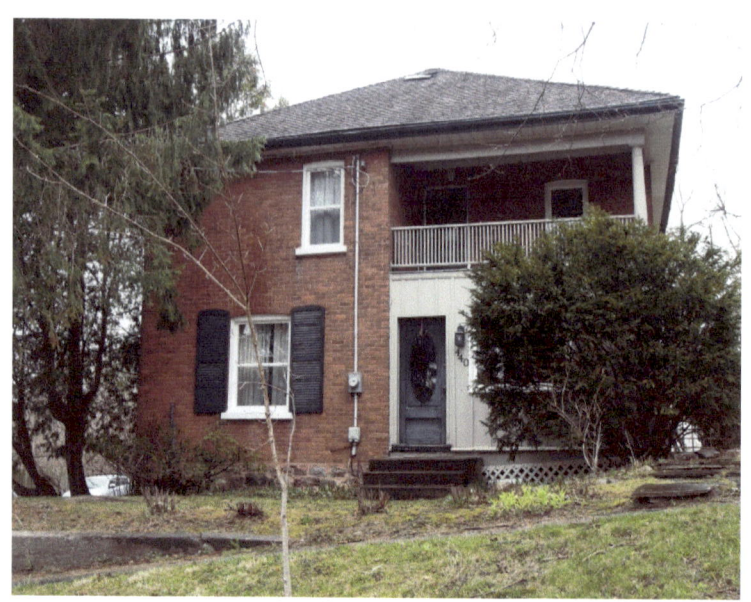

440 Whitevale Road

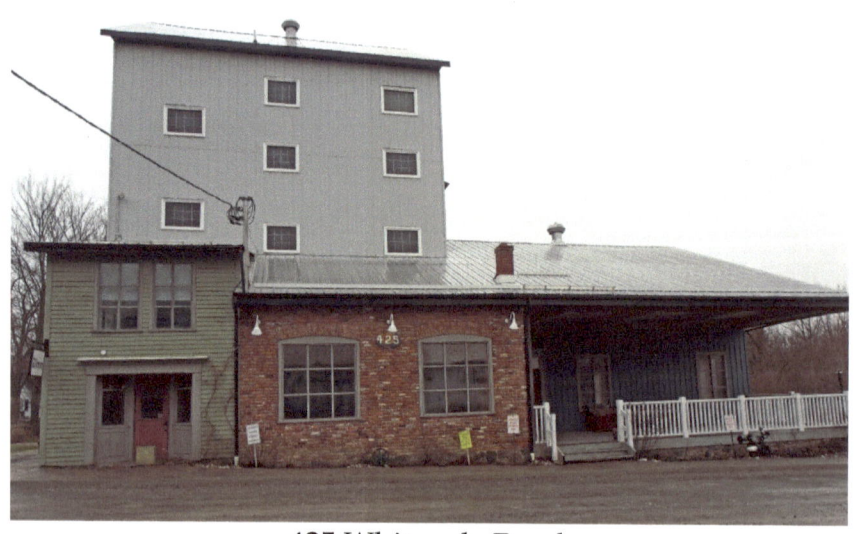

425 Whitevale Road

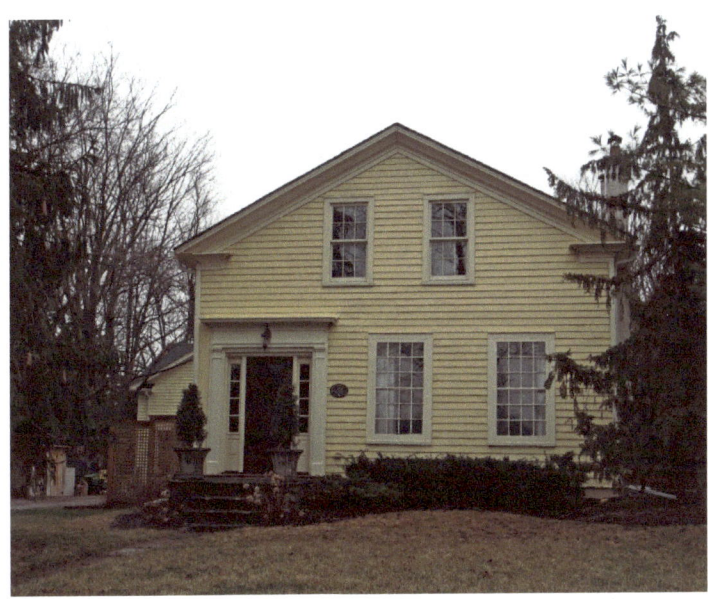

345 Whitevale Road – George Gilchrist, Sash Maker – c. 1858

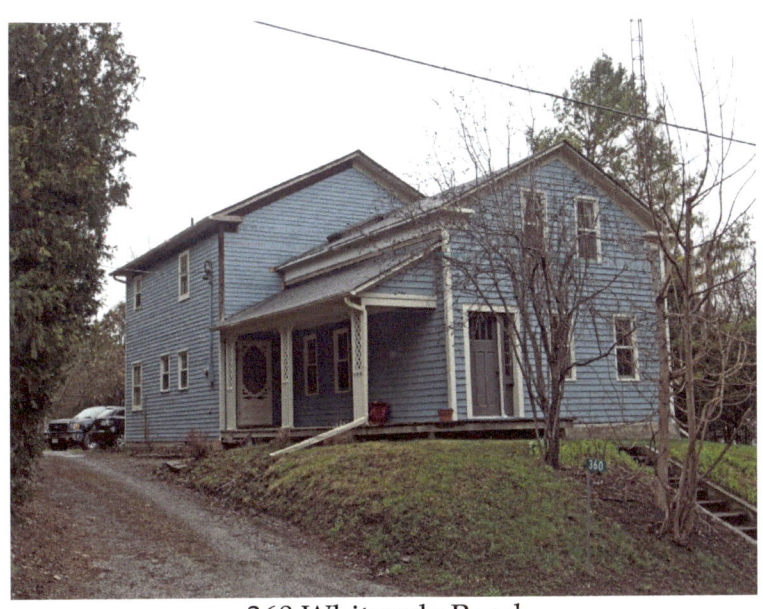

360 Whitevale Road

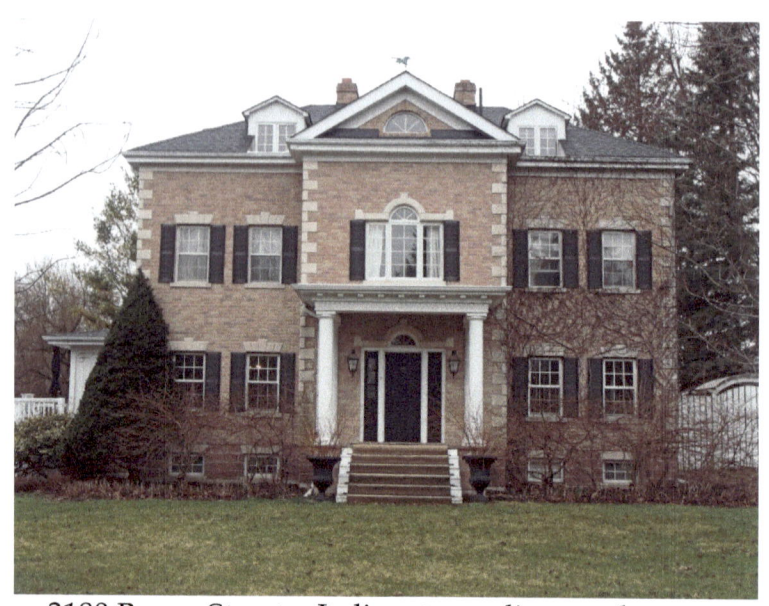

3180 Byron Street – Italianate, pediment, dormers

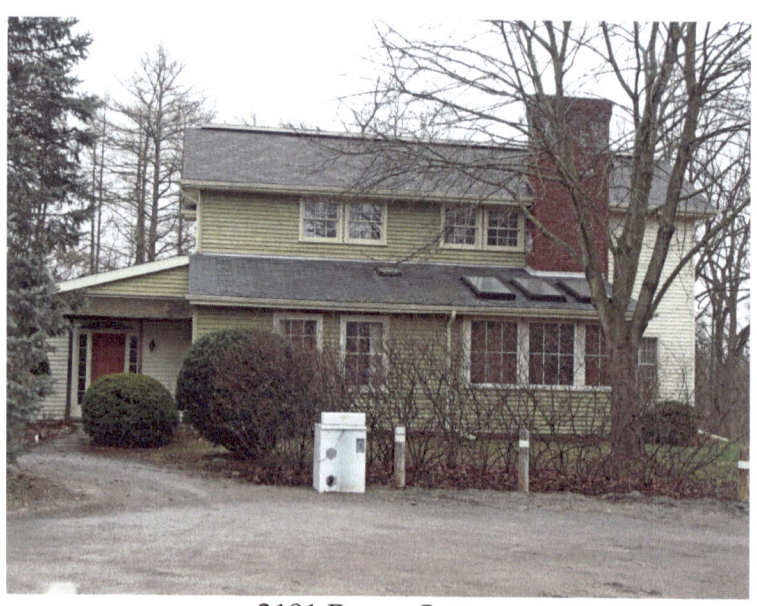

3181 Byron Street

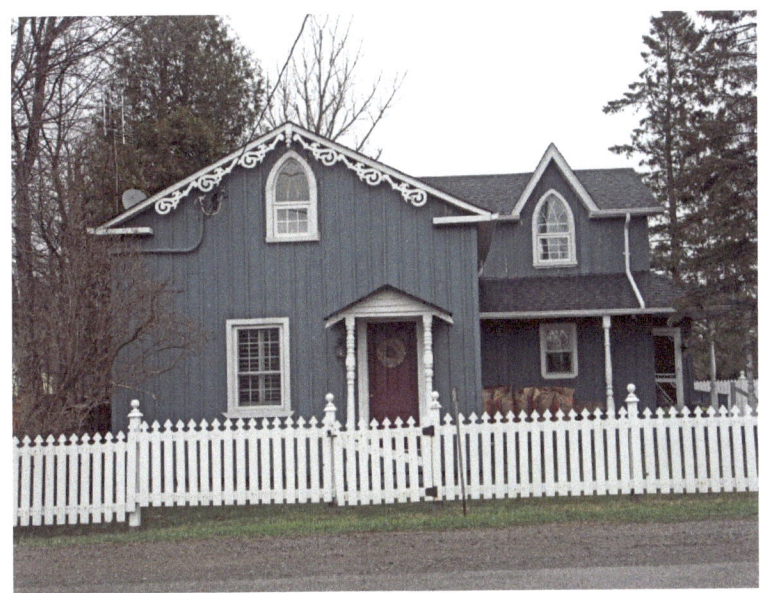

3185 Altona Road – Gothic, verge board trim on gable

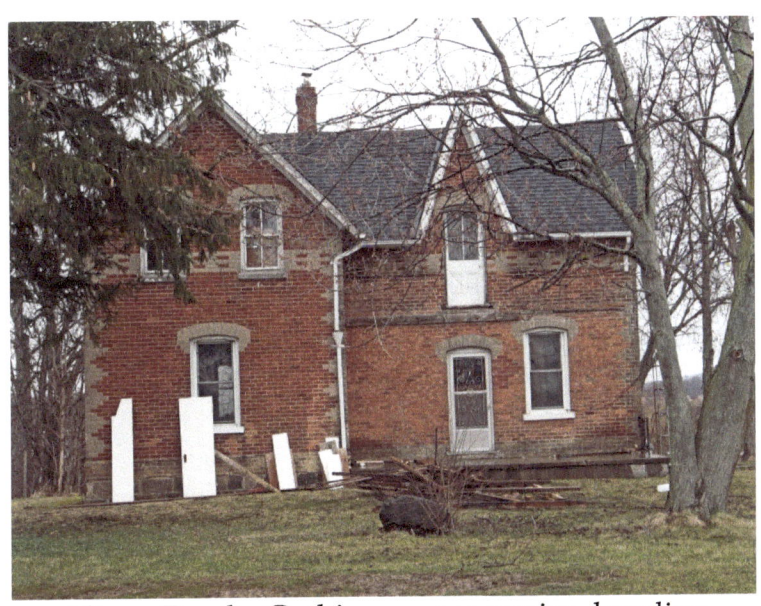

Altona Road – Gothic – corner quoins, banding

Building Styles

Dutch Colonial Revival, 1890-1930 - is distinguished by its gambrel roof, with or without flared eaves, and the frequent use of dormers. The gambrel style allowed an almost complete second floor without the expense of two-story construction. Characteristics: 1½ to 2 stories, clapboard or shingle siding, usually symmetrical facades, gable-end chimneys, round windows in gable end, porch under overhanging eaves, shed, hipped or gable dormers, columns for porches and entry.

Gothic Revival, 1830-1890 – These decorative buildings have sharply-pitched gables with highly detailed verge boards, pointed-arch window openings, and dichromatic brickwork. It is a common style in Ontario.

Italianate, 1850-1900 – A two story rectangular building with a mild hip roof, a projecting frontispiece, and generous eaves with ornate cornice brackets was the basis of the style; often there are large sash windows, quoins, ornate detailing on the windows, belvederes and wraparound verandahs. Italianate commercial buildings often have cast iron cresting and elegant window surrounds.

Italian Villa: This style was the first Ontario style that broke from the architectural traditions of the first settlers and imitated the harmony and balance of Classical architecture found in Northern Italian villas. The style is strictly residential and is characterized by an irregular roofline punctuated by a tall tower or campanile (bell tower). Small balconies, cantilevered eaves offering deep summer shade and arcaded porticos are standard features. Architects designing these houses were clearly after the picturesque.

Neo-Classical, 1810-1850 – This style was a direct result of the War of 1812. Many Upper Canadians returning from the war with the United States were second or third generation Loyalists who had inherited land and means from their forefathers. Once the conflict had passed, they had the money and the time to expand their holdings and indulge their architectural whims. Both residential and commercial buildings were constructed on the traditional Georgian plan, but they had a new gaiety and light-heartedness. Detailing became more refined, delicate, and elegant.

Picturesque is a style of the late 18th and early 19th centuries characterized by a preoccupation with the pictorial values of architecture and landscape in combination with each other. The term picturesque originally denoted a landscape scene that looked as if it came out of a painting in the style of the 17th-century French artists Claude Lorrain or Gaspard Poussin. It was marked by pleasing variety, irregularity, asymmetry, and interesting textures.

Renaissance Revival, 1870-1910 - The Renaissance Palazzo was a three- or four-story building with a rusticated (very large masonry blocks with deep joints and decorated with rough or bold finishes) ground floor, and regularized understated windows on two upper levels, always finished by an elaborate cornice. The Renaissance saw the development of a graceful and balanced adaptation of the Greek styles. In Ontario, the Renaissance was revived in commercial buildings, banks, offices, and churches in many towns. Most of the Renaissance Revival buildings are designed without columns while those with columns and pilasters are more ornate.

Romanesque Revival, 1880-1910 – This style hearkens back to medieval architecture of the 11th and 12th centuries with a heavy appearance, blocky towers and rounded arches.

Tudor Revival – exposed timbers with stucco infill, multi-paned windows.

Vernacular/Traditional Mode 1638 - 1950
Influenced but not defined by a particular style, vernacular buildings are made from easily available materials and exhibit local design characteristics.

Victorian - In Ontario, a Victorian style building can be seen as any building built between 1840 and 1900 that doesn't fit into any of the other categories. It encompasses a large group of buildings constructed in brick, stone, and timber, using an eclectic mixture of Classical and Gothic motifs.

Other Books by Barbara Raue

Coins of Gold
Arrows, Indians and Love
The Life and Times of Barbara
The Cromwell Family Book
Laura Secord Discovered
Daddy Where Are You?

Montana Series
Book 1: Montana Dream
Book 2: Life on the Montana Frontier
Book 3: Montana to Boston and Back
Book 4: Montana Sons Go to War
Book 5: Montana Sons Return from War

Donaldson Series
Book 1: Rite of Passage
Book 2: Rite of Marriage

© 2021 by Barbara Raue - All the photos in this book have been taken with my cameras. I own the rights to them.

Barbara is The Authority on Saving Our History One Photo at a Time. She is pursuing her interest in photography and architecture by preserving a record through photos of old buildings from the 1800s and 1900s with their unique architecture. Enjoy the beautiful architecture in the comfort of your living room. Dream about what it was like in those by-gone days. Dream about what it was like to live in a mansion like one of those in this book.

Barbara Raue, a wife, mother and grandmother, is an avid reader and writer. She has researched and compiled several family histories. In 2010, Barbara published her book "Coins of Gold," which celebrates the courageous life of her mother, May Todd. Barbara's second book is a historical fiction "Arrows, Indians and Love" which takes place in Boonesborough, Kentucky during the time of Daniel Boone. In 2013, Barbara published *The Cromwell Family Book* in which she traces her ancestry generations back into Great Britain. Her second novel is called *Laura Secord Discovered,* in which the story of Laura's service during the War of 1812 is shared. Barbara's memoir is titled *Daddy Where Are You?* It tells of her life growing up without a father. Five novels in the Montana Series have been published, *Montana Dream, Life on the Montana Frontier, Montana to Boston and Back, Montana Sons Go to War,* and *Montana Sons Return from War.* The Donaldson series of two novels is available: *Rite of Passage* and *Rite of Marriage.*

This is a link to Barbara's website to view all of her books
http://barbararaue.ca

www.ingramcontent.com/pod-product-compliance
Lightning Source LLC
Chambersburg PA
CBHW040227220526
45473CB00001B/154